BEAUTY IN THE BEASTS

KRISTIN
VON KREISLER

•

JEREMY P. TARCHER/PUTNAM

a member of Penguin Putnam Inc.

New York

BEAUTY
IN THE
BEASTS

True Stories of
Animals Who Choose
to Do Good

Most Tarcher/Putnam books are available at special quantity
discounts for bulk purchases for sales promotions, premiums,
fund-raising, and educational needs. Special books or book
excerpts also can be created to fit specific needs. For details,
write Putnam Special Markets, 375 Hudson Street,
New York, NY 10014.

Jeremy P. Tarcher/Putnam
a member of
Penguin Putnam Inc.
375 Hudson Street
New York, NY 10014
www.penguinputnam.com

First trade paperback edition 2002
Copyright © 2001 by Kristin von Kreisler
All rights reserved. This book, or parts thereof, may not
be reproduced in any form without permission.
Published simultaneously in Canada

A list of photography credits can be found
at the back of the book

The Library of Congress cataloged the hardback edition as follows:

Von Kreisler, Kristin, date.
Beauty in the beasts : true stories of animals who choose
to do good / Kristin von Kreisler.
p.   cm.
Includes bibliographical references
ISBN 1-58542-093-X
1. Altruistic behavior in animals—Ancedotes.   I. Title.

QL775.5 .V648   2001   00-069071
591.5—dc21
ISBN 1-58542-158-8 (Paperback edition)

Printed in the United States of America

1   3   5   7   9   10   8   6   4   2

This book is printed on acid-free paper. ∞

Book design by Jennifer Ann Daddio

For Martha Hannon,
my beloved friend and mentor.
With many, many thanks.

All his works are beautiful, down to the smallest and faintest spark
  of light.
All these things go on forever, and all of them have their purpose.
All things are in pairs, each the opposite of the other, but nothing
  the Lord made is incomplete.
Everything completes the goodness of something else.
Could anyone ever see enough of this splendor?

—SIRACH 42: 22–25

CONTENTS

FOREWORD

In my talks about animal emotions, I always ask the audience to tell me their favorite books about animals. Sometimes they are the usual classics, like *Black Beauty* or *Watership Down*, and sometimes they are the more modern classics by Jane Goodall and Elizabeth Marshall Thomas, but I was interested to learn that many people in my talks mentioned *The Compassion of Animals*, by Kristin von Kreisler. It is one of my favorite books, too, which is why I wrote a foreword to it. When I ask them why they liked the book so much, they often tell me that it is because it speaks to them in a language they can understand. They do not have to worry that they will be put off by words they do not know, concepts that are strange to them, research that is beyond their comprehension. "It feels," one woman said to me, "like sitting down with a kindly neighbor and having a really deep conversation about animals."

The same is true for this book as well. There is nothing to scare away the reader who feels that science was something left behind in high school. There are many scientific ideas in this book, but they are explained so that anybody, and I really do mean anybody, can immediately understand what they are about. Not only will the ideas be readily understood, but they will make sense: "Oh sure, I have seen that in my dog." Or cat, or bird, or any other animal that we know well. Talk to anybody who lives on close terms with an animal, and you will hear stories about sensitivity and compassion and generosity. But, as Kristin points out, if you go to the large university libraries and try to find books on these topics, they will not be there. You will find many scientific papers on aggression, anger, hostility, fighting, and other negative emotions and behaviors, but you will be hard-pressed to find anything at all in the scientific literature about the topics that Kristin writes about: courage, cooperation, and loyalty. These same scientists, if you talk with them in their living rooms in the evening, will be glad to tell you about some of the amazing things they have seen animals do. They just won't write about it in their scientific books and articles, because they are afraid they will be ridiculed.

But the world is changing, and our attitude toward animals is changing with it. There is a hunger in the general public for true stories of the positive things that animals do. We yearn to learn more about this topic, because we realize that there is a scarcity of human heroes and that perhaps we have been searching in the wrong place. Perhaps it is time to turn to the animals for our soul-therapy, for our moral lessons, for our ethical education. More and more people are beginning to do this, and they are finding that Kristin's first book, and particularly this second one, offers one of the best and most reliable guides to this new and exciting field of human knowledge.

Kristin is careful never to speak of animals as property, to act as if we could possibly own another living being. We are the guardians of some animals, that much is true. But it is equally true that Kristin is among the leaders in a growing field of scholarship where we find that not only do we not own an animal, but that giving up that concept allows a different and deeper kind of friendship. Sometimes animals are our companions on life's difficult journey, sometimes they are our teachers on that same path, but always they are our equals. This profound equality is one of the newest and most exciting ideas around. I am proud to be associated with a pioneer book in this wonderful blossoming world.

—Jeffrey Moussaieff Masson, Ph.D.
Auckland, New Zealand
September 2000

ACKNOWLEDGMENTS

Behind this book are so very many people. I'd like to thank at least a few of them:

My first debt of gratitude goes to Sally Wofford-Girand, my friend and agent, who got me going with her enthusiasm. Then Wendy Hubbert, my supremely insightful editor, took over from there. She was with me every step of the way as I wrote this book, and I have valued her input greatly. Her assistant, Allison Sobel, answered many questions. And my publisher, Joel Fotinos, has allowed this book to grow from concept to reality.

I could never begin to list the hundreds of people who have graciously allowed me to interview them about their animals. But I'd like to acknowledge, at least, some of the experts who took time out from their busy lives to talk with me: Donald Griffin at Harvard University; Margot Lasher at New School University; Bruce Cushing at University of Maryland; David Sloan Wilson at Binghamton University; James Serpell at University of Pennsylvania; Roger Fouts at Central Washington University; Bonnie Beaver at Texas A & M University; Temple Grandin at Colorado State University; Gerald Wilkinson at University of Maryland;

ACKNOWLEDGMENTS

Lee Dugatkin at University of Louisville; Caroline Blanchard at University of Hawaii; Peter Lang at University of Florida; Emily Weiss at Wichita State University; Jon Williams at Kenyon College; Ross Buck at University of Connecticut; Stan Kuczaj at University of Southern Mississippi; Cathy Schaeff at American University; Gordon Burghardt at University of Tennessee; Sally Mendoza at University of California at Davis; Julia Fisher at University of Pennsylvania; Sergio Pellis at University of Lethbridge; Larry Young at Emory University; Daniel Povinelli at University of Southern Louisiana; Con Slobodchikoff at Northern Arizona University; Carel van Schaik at Duke University; Steven Vander Wall at University of Nevada; Tom Lane at University of Florida; Dana Carnegie at Florida's Dolphin Research Center; Ben Hart at University of California at Davis; Bob Andrysco, pet behaviorist in Columbus, Ohio; Sally Blanchard, bird psychologist in Alameda, California; Janet Ruckert, psychologist in Los Angeles, California; Andrew Kallet, DVM, in Corte Madera, California; and Michael Weiss, DVM, in Washington Township, New Jersey.

I'd also like to thank some of my friends and colleagues in the animal-welfare community. They gave advice, references, or material for this book: Leo Grillo at D.E.L.T.A. Rescue; Elliot Katz, Doll Stanley, and Sheri Speede at In Defense of Animals; Dave Johnston at Pets Inc.; Mary Shefferman at *Modern Ferret Magazine*; Karen Davis at United Poultry Concerns; Carrie Hunt at the Wind River Bear Institute; Tim Manley at Montana's Department of Fish, Wildlife and Parks; Mike Lemish at the Vietnam Dog Handlers' Association; Bill Smith at Main Line Rescue; Donna Ewing at the Hooved Animal Humane Society; Fran Sinnot at Lakeshore Animal Friends; John Stokes at the American Eagle Foundation; Jenny Wendel at Dogs with Disabilities; Nancy Furstinger at the Friends of the Delhi Shelter;

Meg Randa at Veganpeace; Liz Baronowski at the Humane Society and S.P.C.A. in Pasadena, California; Kim Shelton at the Humane Society in Raeford, North Carolina; and Tari Hanes, formerly at the Gladstone Animal Shelter in Gladstone, Missouri.

When I was in Africa, other people who are involved with animals in one way or another also helped me find experts for interviews or gave me material for this book: Ronnie Watt, producer of the South African television series "Veldfocus"; Marcella French at South Africa's National Council of S.P.C.A.; Robert Filmer at Eco-Access; Johan Gallant at the Africanish Society of Southern Africa; Arthur Hunt and Lady Isobel Hitz at the Vervet Monkey Foundation; Lorna Stanton at the Bateleur Raptor Rehabilitation Center; Karen Trendler at Wildcare; Louise vander Merwe at *Animal Voice*; Ann Van Dyk at the DeWildt Cheetah Research Center; Johannesburg veterinarian Melvin Greenburg; and animal rehabilitators Stephanie Wolf and Neil Greenwood.

I was delighted to get photographs and videos for this book from Ronnie Watt, Jenny Wendel, Donna Ewing, Judge David Breck, Margaret Smith, Andrea Campbell, Jordan Campbell, Leo Grillo, Jim Bennett, Father Roy Swipes, Kim Rouisse, Glen Herron, Stan Anderson, Kathryn Hollingsworth, Meg Randa, Eleanor Davies, Frances Sinnot, the Los Angeles S.P.C.A., the American Eagle Foundation, Ralston Purina Canada, Heinz Pet Products, and the Monmouth County Sheriff's Department in New Jersey. Jessie Mendez of the U.S. Marines not only sent me a video and photograph but also educated me about military dogs. He kindly gave much of his time and energy to gathering statistics and information for me.

I am grateful to all the hundreds of people who sent letters, faxes, and e-mail messages about their own or other animals.

And Karol Raymer, my good friend, kept mailing newspaper clippings. A number of people at various organizations also alerted me to worthy animals and helped me find their guardians: Christina Dickerson at the Humane Society of Indianapolis; Rick Alampi at the New Jersey Veterinary Medical Association; Bette Morgan at the California Veterinary Medical Association; Jon Becker at the Texas Veterinary Medical Association; David Frei at the Delta Society; and Mary Wamsley, formerly at the Los Angeles S.P.C.A.

By far the majority of the stories in this book came from my friends Kim Bartlett and Merritt Clifton, publisher and editor of *Animal People*. They were incredibly generous about letting me search their files. Then for months Merritt kept sending me more newspaper accounts, so I had the latest and most current examples of animals who choose to do good. I greatly admire Kim and Merritt's dedication to animals and am grateful for their kindness. I'd never even have started this book without their help.

Other friends also offered support that sustained me throughout my work. I'd like especially to thank: Stephanie von Hirschberg, Clell Bryant, Pat Adams, and Scotty and Vicki Erwin for boosting my spirits. Kay Podolsky and Lou and Alice Freund for so generously giving of their expertise with computers and photographs. Irina and Misha Kaluzhinsky for loyally tracking down the articles I couldn't seem to find for myself in Stanford University's libraries. Jeff Masson for inspiring me with his work.

Ray Kilduff encouraged me with his wisdom. Dick Pervier left animal poems on my telephone answering machine every single Friday afternoon to remind me of the beauty and mystery of all creatures. Jimmy Wolf wrote me daily e-mail messages, which were a constant pleasure and comfort during my sometimes lonely writing process.

ACKNOWLEDGMENTS

And, finally, most important, John Bomben, my husband, kept me going. I would like to thank him especially. Without him there would be no book. As my partner in life for so many years, he has given me more support, kindness, and love than I can ever say. I never cease being grateful for his presence in my life.

BEAUTY IN THE BEASTS

INTRODUCTION

My husband, John, and I are constantly taking in desperate animals. They show up, troubled and downtrodden, and we feel morally bound to care for them. As a result, our house is often in an uproar as an animal calms down, works out its problems, and joins our family. John and I can't take credit for the healing. It comes on silent wings and does its work. But it always comes.

Noble

Noble, our German shepherd, was given to us by a friend, who had gotten him from an elderly woman. She could not keep him because at a lively seven months, he kept galloping around the house and knocking her down. We didn't exactly want a moose in our house either, but we had just lost our fifteen-year-old German shepherd and felt a terrible void in our hearts. So we went to meet the dog, a drop-dead handsome pup with fur so sleek and shiny that no one could resist him. He was a galumphing teenager with floppy ears and awkward paws, like mitts.

Though we were well aware that he had been turned out of his house for being a thug, we brought the dog home; and with high hopes we named him Noble. He did not live up to his name. For the first two months, he chased his tail. Nonstop. He stood in the middle of the room and circled around like a maniac, yipping frantically, as if he were trying to converse with the furry tip that eternally eluded him.

John and I could not get through to him. His only way of communicating was through his teeth, by endless chewing: the rug fringe, dining room table legs, upholstered chair pillows. We finally figured out that the little old lady had cruelly locked him up all by himself for days with no toys. His tail was his only friend.

There were months in his first few years with us when we wished that we could banish him, especially on bath days. At the whisper of "bath," Noble tore into our bedroom and wriggled his one-hundred-ten-pound body under the bed, where he thought we could not find him. Of course, we always did. Together, John and I gripped his collar and with gritted teeth dragged him down the hall to the tub, where we pushed him from behind, his legs stiff as planks, his toenails digging into the tile floor.

All through the bath he sulked, shivered, glowered, and deliberately shook his body to shower us with water. John had to wrestle with him to keep him from leaping out of the tub and charging down the hall to hide, soapy and slippery, under the bed. But slowly Noble grew out of being a hooligan. He seemed to agree that he needed to live up to his name, and we stopped referring to him as the Noble Savage. With adoring eyes, he followed John around and loyally lay between our feet at dinner, almost as if he were trying in his own way to pay us back for befriending him.

One morning, with the usual apprehension on Noble's bath days, John went to get the swimming trunks he always wore in self-defense for combat with him in the tub. Noble, lying on his cushion, watched John lift the trunks out of the drawer; then Noble disappeared. We searched behind the living room sofa, under the dining table, in the corner of the laundry room. No Noble. And it was no small feat for a moose-sized dog to go undetected in our small house.

I went to the bathroom to get Noble's towels and shampoo out of the closet. There, sitting in the tub, looking beatific, was Noble. He didn't glance at me but gazed at the soap dish, his mind seeming to be on another plane reserved for dogs who carry out heroic feats. His expression was not so much of resignation, but of dignity. With great elegance and courage, he was waiting for his bath.

To this day, whenever John goes to get his swimming trunks to give Noble a bath, Noble climbs into the tub. Sometimes Noble gets into the tub *before* John opens the drawer for his trunks, when all John has done is *think* that it's Noble's bath time. John has even tried to trick him by going swimming in the morning and coming home, still in his trunks, to give the bath. But Noble always knows: John finds him waiting in the tub.

John believes that Noble reads his mind. I believe that Noble wants to please him. For us, on bath days Noble goes against his desperate wish to avoid water, shelves his own needs, and does what he hates for the sake of family harmony. In those moments, Noble chooses to be cooperative.

Some of you may be thinking, "Hold on. Wait a minute. Stop right there." I can guess what's on your mind: "Cooperation? From a dog? Isn't cooperation a human trait?"

Yes, you're right. It is. But it's also one of many sterling traits that animals, as well as humans, have. Animals can, and do, in fact, *choose* to do good, just as Noble did. In addition to cooperation, they can choose to show courage, loyalty, resourcefulness, fortitude, and many other exemplary qualities.

Once I realized that animals were capable of the same admirable traits that we humans usually reserve for ourselves, I

Beatrice

started looking for those traits in animals around me. I found them all the time. In fact, I began to see animals in a whole new light; Noble's cooperation was just the tip of the iceberg. I was amazed by animals' huge potential for goodness when they are free to choose it.

I thought of Bea.

One warm autumn night as John and I walked along our road in the moonlight, a streak of mottled brown, black, and white passed in front of us so quickly in the shadows that we could hardly tell it was a dog. But it was one, Bea, clearly lost, we realized, as she ran up and down driveways, frantically looking for something but never finding it. Thinking we would locate her family the next morning, we chased her down and brought her home.

Under the kitchen light, however, we saw that we could never give her back. Bea was scruffy and malnourished, a ragamuffin with dark tear stains in the fur beneath her eyes. When she walked, her breasts swung from side to side, like a pendulum, sagging so low that her teats brushed the floor. She refused to acknowledge us in any way. In fact, when I tried to pet her, she shrank back to avoid my hand and vibrated. Terror seemed to emanate from her in curly waves.

As I tried to calm her, I stroked her ears and discovered a tattooed ID number inside one of them. During calls the next day to the Humane Society and the American Kennel Club, I learned that she had been tattooed at a medical lab and was an experimental beagle, who had somehow gotten free. Now I understood why she was so afraid.

For months John and I lived with a vibrating beagle. Worse, whenever he—or any man—came close to her, she rolled on her back, raised her legs in the air, and urinated in submission. A psychiatrist might have looked at her, thought of a dog's version of Auschwitz or the Gulag Archipelago, and diagnosed post-traumatic stress. She was at her most terrorized whenever I took her to our veterinarian, Andrew.

On the first visit, Andrew, in his white coat with his stethoscope around his neck, opened the door of the exam room. Before he even took a step inside, Bea took one look at him and shook so hard that I was scared she'd have a heart attack. When Andrew came closer, she threw herself onto her back, urinated, and curled into a pill bug's ball of self-defense, her eyes clamped shut to block him out, her nose pressed hard against her tail.

Andrew was supremely kind and understanding, but he was also a realist. "She's been used and abused," he pointed out, as Bea continued trembling like an aspen leaf. "Sometimes lab animals never come around as pets. You have to be prepared for that. If things don't work out, you've got to be ready to give up and let her go."

Andrew's words, like a Greek chorus' warning, cropped up in my mind constantly for the first six months Bea lived with us. We worried endlessly that she was more than we could handle, that she'd never be a normal dog. But slowly she grew plump and glossy. Then, so gradually that we barely noticed, she shook less intensely and for a shorter time when John came near her — and eventually she tolerated his petting. After a couple of years, she followed us around like a little sentinel. She had learned to love.

One afternoon I braced myself for the inevitable stress of taking her to Andrew for her annual checkup. As we waited in the exam room, the clinic smells must have reminded Bea of her sorry past. Clearly feeling that she was back in hostile territory, she paced the tile floor and panted nervously. After every pass around the steel examination table, she stopped and inhaled deep breaths at the crack under the door, as if she were reassuring herself about an escape route. No one could deny that her old fears had resurfaced, but she was dealing with them, like an agoraphobic inching bravely across the threshold of her house.

Andrew opened the door and came into the room. Bea stopped pacing and looked warily up at him, but she did not roll on her back and urinate. When he picked her up and set her on the steel table, she panted a few more nervous pants, then withdrew her tongue and clamped her mouth shut. He pressed his stethoscope against her heart. "Fluttering," he said.

Aside from an occasional, uncontrollable shiver working its way down Bea's neck to her tail, her fear would have been her secret. She stood there, her legs straight and strong, her head high, her tail raised in the cheerful "flag" that beagles are known for. As Andrew thumped her stomach and curled back her lips to examine her teeth, she did not cower or resist. Everything about her was dignified, even gracious.

At that moment Bea had overcome no telling how much trauma and terror. Maybe it can even be said that she'd given up grudges and had forgiven what had been done to her. Who can say? But one thing was sure: She was fighting her fears of men in white lab coats, and she was winning the fight. She was choosing to be courageous.

Overcoming so much to behave with such bravery was a dramatic turnaround, a real moral victory for Bea. As I kept thinking about ways that animals could choose to do good, I realized that exemplary behavior didn't always have to be so extraordinary. It could also be more quiet and subtle.

And what could be more subtle than cats? They, too, can decide to act with decency, I came to realize. My cat William—whom I fondly call William Goodcat—is an example. He's a swaggering tomcat with chest puffed out and nicks in his ears from victorious fights, like notches in a six-shooter. When he

William

walks into a room, he commands it. He is Clint Eastwood spitting out the challenge, "Make my day."

When John and I first found William, though, he was not the swaggering tough guy that he is now. A feral cat, splotched brown and black and white—like a little pinto pony—he was sitting, his shoulders hunched to protect his chest, underneath the bird feeder in our yard. His pink tongue hung from his mouth as he panted dismally and shook the involuntary shakes that come with severe pain.

We knew that something terrible was wrong with him but also that he was wild and we'd never be able to catch him and take him to Andrew. For two days the cat hung around the garden like a wounded bird until I could no longer bear to watch him suffer. Determined at least to try to do what I could for him, I went to the Humane Society and rented a trap, which I set in the bushes and baited with canned gourmet tuna feast.

The next morning, I found William, hissing and yowling through the cage bars, furious at his incarceration. Even though he was so sick, he wanted nothing more than a giant bite out of me—and of Andrew, who anesthetized him, made an incision in his chest, and discovered that his diaphragm was ripped open. He'd probably been the victim of a hit-and-run driver.

Andrew left him on the operating table and called me on the phone. "Are you *sure* you want me to go ahead with this?" he kept asking. "He needs expensive surgery. I can always put him down." Even though I hardly knew William, I couldn't let him die. Most of my secret savings went to his surgery; large chunks of my next few days went to visiting him, conked out in a cage, too pitiful and weak to protest my petting.

But then William started feeling better. I brought him home and opened his cage, but he did not dash off into the woods and disappear, as I'd expected. Instead, he stalked into the bushes, where he sulked in the foliage until the next morning when he appeared for the breakfast I always put on the porch for the other feral cats. That established our routine: my feeding, him eating — with no love lost between us, as far as he was concerned.

Any time he got close enough for me to touch him while I doled out food, I did. At every touch, he shot off the porch like a cannonball. One day he hesitated maybe an eighth of a second before his escape; another day he shrank back only a few steps. Slowly our friendship progressed so far that he stiffened up and endured my petting without shrinking back at all.

After five years William was tame — and even loving. Whenever I came home, he ran out of the bushes and down the steps to greet me, then escorted me to the front door, where I stroked his head and complimented him on his buck fangs. Beneath the macho lion was a gentle soul, who came into the house one day and stood in the living room as if he were formally announcing a change in status. From then on, inside most of the time, he draped himself with grace across sofas and chairs and snuggled up to my feet in bed.

Except one night, when John left town on business. William, instead of going to his spot at the foot of the bed, slowly advanced to John's pillow, where he settled into his chicken position, feet tucked under his body, his little face so close to mine that his whiskers tickled my cheeks. William purred like a diesel engine, a purr so comforting that I quickly fell asleep, unusual for me when I am home alone, imagining burglars staking out the house to get my grandmother's silver pitcher. When I opened my eyes the next morning, I found William still keeping vigil over me. If a burglar *had* broken into the house and come close to the bed, I have no doubt that William would have sprung on him and shredded him to ribbons.

Now whenever John is gone, William takes up his guard post

on the pillow—his favorite spot though he could choose others. I'm certain he's trying to help me get through the night in peace. Just as I felt compelled to take care of him when he arrived so injured twelve years ago, he seems to feel the same for me when I'm alone and insecure. Perhaps he is trying to live up to a role he's assigned to himself as a watchcat. William is choosing to be loyal.

I tell these stories to illustrate what I believe is my animals' choosing goodness. John and I are not responsible for the choice. Each of these animals had to overcome insecurity and fear, and they did it quietly, at their own pace, with no prodding from us. Then, independently, they spun their excellent behavior out of themselves. Somewhere along the line, they changed their attitude and decided to act as they did.

Perhaps the animals were showing gratitude and trying to pay us back for our efforts to save them. Or maybe they'd been living with us long enough to decide that they should measure up and behave in ways that would please us. They might also have felt that the time had come to be helpful and considerate, to stop causing trouble, or to contribute what they could to family harmony. Or they might simply have wanted to be decent just for the sake of decency. Who knows?

Whatever their reason, they made a choice to act differently than they had before. On their own, without being asked or forced, they were showing goodness; you could even call it virtue. To me, goodness, or virtue, means right action and impeccable behavior. It means displaying commendable qualities—such as cooperation, courage, and loyalty—which are all abstract nouns that need active, freely chosen verbs to bring them to life. Goodness also implies a moral sense of right and wrong, an expectation of how one should be treated or should treat others with fairness, helpfulness, and sympathy. I believe that all animals, and not just mine, can have this moral sense and, more important, that they can act on it to show benevolence.

I became completely convinced of animals' capacity for it ten years ago, after an earthquake, measuring 7.1 on the Richter scale, rocked my house. All alone and too frightened to sleep indoors that night, I set out a sleeping bag on my patio and laid pillows on the concrete for Ludwig, my German shepherd at the time; Tigger, my tabby cat; and Beatrice.

I was grateful for the presence of my animals, but I was still terrified by the constant trembling of aftershocks. As I lay there, shivering and feeling as if I were the only person left alive on the planet, my animals seemed to recognize my distress. Just as William had come to sleep next to me when John was away, one by one, my animals got up from their comfortable pillows and walked over to me. Ludwig lay on the concrete and curled his body protectively around my head. Tigger snuggled up in the crook behind my knees. Bea rooted down into my sleeping bag and rested her head on my neck so close that I could smell her gentle breath.

I was certain that the animals had seen how badly I needed reassurance, and they had come to offer it. Though I'd lived with animals all my life, only that night, surrounded by their love and kindness, did I realize that animals could show compassion. I was so moved by it that I began looking for other examples of similar behavior and quickly collected hundreds of stories from publications and from animal organizations. I knew I was onto something important, and, in fact, I began to see animal kindness everywhere, almost as a force on the earth, like gravity.

I wrote a book about it, *The Compassion of Animals*. In the months after publication, readers' letters about their own animals arrived in a deluge. Then came almost daily faxes and

e-mails from other people who wanted to share personal incidents or newspaper accounts. When I read all the stories, I realized that animals behave with far more admirable traits than just
compassion. They show goodness in many other ways.

I also came to understand that the fine behavior is not acci-
dental, haphazard, or unconscious, and that behind each incident
of goodness is choice. During an interview several years ago with
Marc Bekoff, a biology professor at the University of Colorado,
we talked about a stray cat who'd given her all to help a dog.
Marc said, "The cat didn't *have* to do it. She chose to." That
observation about deliberate choice struck me like a lightning
bolt and became the seed for this book.

O f course, I'm well aware that all animals do not choose to
do good. People have pointed out to me, for instance, pit
bulls who act like Jeffrey Dahmer or Hitler cats who take
delight in torturing mice. Having seen my share of those dogs
and cats, I do not intend to idealize all animals, with one senti-
mental, broad-brush sweep, as innocent and incorruptible. On
the contrary, I believe that animals, like people, choose to behave
in all gradations of decency from nasty to angelic.

An example is a chimpanzee, rescued by Karen Trendler at
Wildcare, an animal rehabilitation center in Pretoria, South
Africa. The chimp would normally put his hand through his wire
cage to grab his daily fruit except when Trendler's husband fed
him. Then the chimp would slowly pull his hand farther and farther back into the cage to lure the man's to follow. Once his hand
was through the bars, the chimp trounced on it and held him
there, perhaps to retaliate for the confines of captivity—or
maybe simply to be mean.

In contrast, I've read of a gorilla who watched a zookeeper

smoking and made little cigarettes out of paper and hay, which he generously gave to her as gifts. And I've heard about chimps cleaning another chimp's wounds, licking the blood, shooing flies away, and traveling slowly, so the injured chimp could keep up. Then there's the famous Binti Jua, a gorilla at a Brookfield, Illinois zoo. After a child fell into her enclosure, she picked him up, cradled and protected him, and kindly handed him over to zoo officials. Obviously, not all primates, any more than all humans, can be lumped together. They choose whether they'll be mean or kind.

The same goes for elephants. They've been seen swinging their trunks in a la-dee-da, casual sort of way, all seeming innocence. Then on a downward swing, the elephants snatch a comrade's hay, an act of sly thievery and pure disloyalty. Yet the documentary *Reflections on Elephants* shows how, after a baby died in a drought, elephants from miles around stopped to console its mother—with obvious compassion and empathy. And in *Elephant Memories*, Cynthia Moss describes two elephants' desperate attempt to prop up a third, shot in the lungs by poachers and sinking to the ground. Even after she died, blood gushing from her mouth, the two frantically tried to lift her to a sitting position. One broke a tusk and suffered great pain by choosing to try so hard to help.

Even birds can choose their place along the broad spectrum of behavior. Ninety percent of them were always thought to be monogamous, mostly because they stick together to raise their brood. However, recent genetic fingerprinting revealed that, nearly a third of the time, males are feeding and tending babies in the nest who are not theirs. Many mother birds, in other words, have dalliances with other males, then lay eggs of mixed paternity. So much for loyalty in birds.

But there was also an exemplary female Canada goose, who

took up residence with her mate one winter in Joanne Ogburn's yard on Irondequoit Bay near Rochester, New York. Ogburn named the birds Lucy and Herman and wondered why they had dropped out of their flock instead of continuing south to a more hospitable climate. When the weather turned colder, ice formed on their beaks, and the geese began to starve. Ogburn bought them a bag of millet, and her children set out soft rags on the breezeway, where the birds nested for three weeks.

One evening Herman walked out onto the ice in the middle of the bay and plopped down. Lucy waddled to the shore and sat down, too, unsheltered in the snow, where she watched him for two long, freezing days and nights—until he died. Ogburn finally understood why he and Lucy had left their flock and stopped there. Lucy had chosen cold and hardship in order to stay with her sick mate until the end. Only when spring came did she finally fly away. An example of exquisite, freely chosen bird loyalty.

Last year I interviewed Ben Hart, chief of behavioral science at the University of California at Davis's Veterinary Medical Teaching Hospital. I told him about the newspaper account of Minnie, who, I believed, had chosen to be undeniably generous.

Minnie was a pathetic, bedraggled, and filthy mutt, so thin that underneath her fur was a little picket fence of ribs. A stray, she was also starved for affection. She walked up to David Bruce and his two-year-old son on the street in Hayward, California, and stood beside them, seeming to ask to be petted.

When Bruce bent down and stroked her dirty ears, his son was so eager to befriend her that he begged to be let out of his stroller. So Bruce set him on the sidewalk. Thinking that his son was surely safe around her, Bruce bent down to tie his shoelace.

Suddenly the child dashed into the street—right in front of a speeding car.

Before Bruce could straighten up and run after his child, Minnie tore into the street and pushed the boy out of the way, just as the car screeched to a stop exactly where he had been standing. Minnie saved the boy's life. She chose to risk her own life for a total stranger. She might easily have wound up dead.

"Why did she do that?" I asked Professor Hart. "Why would a stray dog put herself out like that to help someone she didn't even know?"

"Maybe the dog thought the boy had food and ran to get it and didn't see the car," he said.

As I prodded him for other ways of looking at Minnie's action, he suggested that I'd been mistaken about the story I'd just told him, and that she'd probably not saved the boy at all.

"This story may have been embellished. You need to talk with an eyewitness and ask, 'What did you see?' You've got to find out what *really* went on," he warned.

Furthermore, even if Minnie had tried to save the boy, no one could call her behavior "compassionate," he added. "It's difficult to attribute that quality to animals. You don't have verbal reporting from them to give that explanation."

No matter how Hart looked at Minnie, she lost. He dismissed her kindness, bravery, and generosity, and all because of that niggling issue, "verbal reporting." Because animals can't talk to explain in *words* why they do what they do, many scientists refuse to consider animals' feelings and motives and ignore what animals tell us by their actions.

Actually, it's no wonder many researchers are reluctant to acknowledge that animals can choose to do good. For one thing, scientific experiments are rarely set up to see positive animal behavior. In a psychological literature database at Stanford University, I found 1,130 citations for animal fear but only one for animal courage. To say the least, research topics seem to indicate a bias against animals being shown in a positive light.

For another thing—and experiments aside—most scientists would probably never have the chance in labs to see animals carry out the spontaneous acts of goodness that I have found in my research. Lab animals lead extremely difficult lives and are usually caged, treated at best with indifference, and have little or no bond to the people who experiment with them. As a result, they can't dive bravely into rivers to save someone or walk loyally for hundreds of miles to find their human families. Lab animals have neither the freedom nor the incentive to choose to do good.

When scientists hear anecdotes of such behavior in non-lab animals, they tend to consider the incidents meaningless, one-time oddities of behavior that prove nothing about goodness, choice, or anything else—because the behavior could not be reproduced under controlled conditions in experiments. Yet I believe that all the anecdotes I've collected of animals choosing to do good add up. The sum is not a random pile of insignificant stories, but data, which prove my point. Providing that proof is what I hope to do in this book.

I also hope to show where our own morality may have come from. I believe that it has stemmed from the animals who lived before us, that we're all, animal and human, extensions of the same life force and part of one great soup of awareness. We share basic impulses, strivings, feelings, and what Carl Jung called the universal unconscious. Yet scientists have told me that such thinking is a sure sign of the "Bambi complex" or blatant anthropomorphism, meaning that I'm attributing human qualities to animals and projecting my own motives and emotions onto them. These scientists claim that animals intend absolutely nothing by their actions, that animals "sleepwalk" through life on "automatic pilot" without even being consciously *aware* of what they do, much less able to make choices about their behavior. Animals, in other words, wander around like robots in a perpetual muddle.

What's so discouraging about this argument is that it negates animals' extraordinary determination, resilience, sensitivity, kindness, and hard work. It also pits all beings against each other, "us" versus "them." The "us" is capable of choosing goodness and fine behavior. The "them" is not.

Yet we've evolved from animals. Our flesh, bones, cells, and even brain nerve tissue all look and work like those of other species. Surely it's not the case that at some point in evolution, only we humans suddenly had a great flash of enlightenment and became capable of decency while animals lagged behind in darkness as malevolent wretches. Studies of skeletons in Los Angeles's La Brea tar pits have revealed that even prehistoric, saber-toothed tigers fed and cared for other tigers who had debilitating injuries and chronic illnesses. We can't be so arrogant as to believe that goodness and morality started only with us—especially when so many animals all around us also seem to show a sense of right and wrong.

If we're willing to look, we can see in animals what I believe may be the rudiments of our own human ethical code. How many of us, for example, have scolded our dogs and watched them shrink back with dark looks on their faces—and with what absolutely seems like a guilty conscience? Arthur Hunt, who started South Africa's Vervet Monkey Foundation, witnessed the basics of animal justice when some young monkeys ganged up, chased, and bit a weaker one; and Whitey, an eighteen-year-old female, pulled them off by the hair of their heads and smacked them to stop the unfair harassment.

Animals can also act almost like conscientious good citizens, patrolling the neighborhood and looking out for the needy: The golden retriever of Connecticut talk-show host David Smith woke him in the middle of the night and led him to the goldfish bowl to show him that a fish had jumped out and was lying, desperate for help, on the floor. Even wildlife can seem to show a basic sense of ethics. Supremely responsible wolves, for instance, act as if they value community interests above individual ones, as we're encouraged to do. The wolves submit to others of higher rank in their pack, share food, care for the young and infirm, and defend their territories with the zeal of patriotic soldiers.

All these animals are exhibiting a simple, stripped down, bare-bones form of morality when they choose to help or keep order or look after others. My pointing this out may not be so much anthropomorphic as empathic. In this book I am trying to understand from animals' behavior what motives and feelings might be in their heads.

In the process of trying to understand, I believe we can learn much from animals about goodness and morality. Animals can set examples for us. Those examples can nourish us and give us hope while we try to get by in a world that, for many, is rapidly becoming a moral desert, a place where we are starved for heroes. I don't know about you, but I get queasy when I read about athletes biting off ears, movie stars being arrested with prostitutes, politicians of both parties facing seemingly endless trials for moral lapses. I'm often hungry for someone to look up to. I keep needing to feel that absolutes, like truth and goodness, exist somewhere.

Though heroes and mentors can seem few and far between, for me, filling in that gap are the special animals I have known or come upon in my research. When the sound of clay feet becomes deafening, I look to these animals' simple, nonverbal world for comfort and inspiration. Their goodness doesn't necessarily make glittering headlines. Usually, it is subtle and easily missed if we aren't looking. But it's there—as an animal's one single moment of triumph, or as its many simple acts of decency, strung out day after day throughout its life.

Recently I asked Kim Bartlett, publisher of *Animal People*, if she had seen any of her cats choose to do good. Immediately, her face brightened, and she told me about Bull, a big orange feral tom with white, jail-suit stripes and ears, battle-scarred as a pirate's.

When Bartlett and her husband, Merritt Clifton, were picking up homeless cats for a rescue project, a woman told them about a feral tom who had gently led two tiny kittens to her door, meowed, and looked up at her with eager eyes that begged her to feed the babies.

"You don't mean a tomcat," Bartlett corrected the woman. "You mean a feral *mother*." No tom on earth would nurture kittens, Bartlett believed.

She was wrong. The tom turned out to be Bull, who was living in a wrecked, abandoned car in the slums of Shelton, Connecticut. All winter, he'd been helping the kittens survive the bitter cold. Besides being an exemplary father, he was also a model of kindness.

After Bartlett trapped him and brought him home to live with forty other feral cats she was taming for adoption, he quickly settled in. If any cat was picking on another, Bull stood beside the weaker one and stared down the assaulter until it slunk away. Without hissing or fighting, Bull bravely offered his protection.

Sometimes he groomed the other cats. They followed him around and took turns sleeping next to him. He waited his turn at the communal feeding bowls, then generously left food behind for the others. Whenever he started coughing up a hairball, he ran to the litter box. Bartlett is convinced that he did this out of consideration, so as not to mess the floor.

If she was sad or distressed, Bull came and sat beside her. Though he darted away, skittish, if she tried to touch him, he stayed close until her bad mood passed. He recognized her pain, she believes, and wanted to do what he could for her. "He was truly a noble soul," she says. "He would have been moral by human standards."

Animals can also be moral by *animal* standards. They can demonstrate sterling behavior and traits when they choose. Sometimes I think that one of the main purposes of the animals who come into our lives is to teach us about decency, as Bull did for Bartlett.

Some animals try so hard. When they do, we need to see it and acknowledge the beauty and the goodness of their actions. The stories in this book are meant to give credit where credit is due.

1.

SENSITIVITY

I remember the first time I saw wild elephants. Massive and wrinkled, the creatures were standing around in a small group, decimating a tree. As they chomped on bark and branches, the tree changed in a matter of minutes from a flourishing, growing thing to a telephone pole. It never had a chance against those hungry, lumbering creatures.

I was particularly struck by the elephants' trunks. Used for yanking, tugging, and ripping apart foliage, the trunks had a fire hose's strength and toughness. And yet, as the elephants also gently skimmed the delicate tips of their trunks along branches to search for the right spot to grab, I thought of ballerinas' graceful hands. I realized that those hulking, thick-skinned elephants, who could have squashed me flat with one stomp of a foot, were also supremely sensitive.

But I wasn't aware of just *how* sensitive they were. I later learned that when a female mates for the first time, other cows in her all-female herd gather around to calm and reassure her. With their bodies they even support the bull's weight—usually more than twice as much as hers—to keep him from hurting her when he places his front feet on her back to mount her. Later, while she gives birth, her female herd-mates surround her again to encourage and console her. They greet the new baby with soft touches of their trunks.

All the females in the herd nurture and protect the young, a phenomenon called "allomothering." Caring trunks constantly caress each baby; an adult is always around to meet its needs. When a female gets old and infirm, the other members of her group stay with her and offer help and comfort until she dies. Beneath their tough hides, elephants can be gentle souls.

Their sensitivity is hard to come by in our world. It is a concerned attentiveness based on empathy, meaning one understands the feelings and experiences of another and is moved by them. Once you get an idea of what it's like to walk in another's shoes, you have a choice, and that's when the morality of empathy becomes apparent. You can choose to turn your back and walk away, just as a dog who's been abused and trusts no one might do. Or you can get in sync and share what the other is going through. You can sympathize, connect, and comfort. Most important, you can care.

Female elephants seem to do this when they respond so gently to their sisters. So do other animals—interacting with their own kind or with other species, including us. The empathy depends on "attunement," as Margot Lasher explained to me. Soft spoken and gentle herself, she teaches in the social sciences department at New York City's New School University and writes about the human-animal bond.

Attunement—or empathy—happens "when an animal tunes into another's quality of energy and resonates it," Lasher says. "When you get upset, animals can feel the 'upsetness' because of the connection they have with you." If the connection is close and trusting, it ties you together, almost as if a rope joined your hearts. When your emotions tug the rope, the animal feels the tugging and is pulled to you. This goes both ways. Whatever affects one of you affects the other.

People often close themselves off from their emotions and upsetness. Because of our culture, for instance, men often feel that they can't be fearful; women, that they can't get mad. But animals don't block any of their feelings or close themselves off from ours. "Animals will always stay open," Lasher says, especially in times of trouble.

When something is wrong, animals sense it and often choose to stay in tune with us until they figure out what's going on and how to help. Then, by resting their head in our lap or cuddling up at our feet, they show they understand and are tied to us. "From an animal's openness and connection comes a feeling of closeness and concern that is calming and comforting," says Lasher.

The most important result of animal empathy is that comforting, which, I believe, can almost do more for us than any dramatic physical actions animals might take on our behalf. Their awareness of how we feel can be immensely healing. Their empathy is like balm.

An animal's sensitivity is usually just a quiet, simple gesture. And yet it can be nothing short of stunning. Here are a few examples:

In a Renton, Washington, emergency vet care clinic, Perkins, a seventeen-year-old orange tabby, was diagnosed with cancer. The vet recommended putting Perkins down because he also had heart disease and kidney failure. Perkins's family, Jamie Hicks and her brother, hugged the cat and cried. They couldn't bear to think of losing him forever. Each second with him before he died was precious, and Perkins seemed to understand their sadness. So weak and sick, he still managed to raise his head and with his sandpaper tongue gently licked away their tears and consoled them. "I believe he knew it was his time to go, and he was ready," says Jamie Hicks. "He did everything he could to make it easier for us."

Yippo, a Great Dane, also tried to make things easier for his guardian, Jo McCubbins, who was extremely uncomfortable in her eighth month of pregnancy. Yippo seemed to understand that months of morning sickness and exhaustion had made Jo sick and tired, and that she was tired of feeling that way. All she wanted was for her baby to hurry up and come into the world.

Raised as a fraternity mascot at the University of Southern California, "Yippo was always a perfect gentleman," says Mc-Cubbin, who lives in Sweet Home, Oregon. "It was like he always knew just what to do." And he did it one afternoon when Mc-Cubbins parked her car in front of a laundromat and dragged out the laundry, bundled in a sheet that she had tied into a knot on top. Holding the huge load over her huge belly, she struggled toward the door.

Yippo saw Jo's difficulty and frustration. He seemed to know that she was feeling overwhelmed. Grabbing the sheet's knot in his teeth, he took the clumsy burden from her. Because the bundle was so big and heavy, he had to rear his head far back to keep the laundry off the ground. But, like a stork carrying a baby, he lugged the sheet and all its contents into the laundromat, where customers rewarded his astounding sensitivity with cheers.

Another astoundingly sensitive dog was an elderly, arthritic mutt in Lebanon, Wisconsin. Many years ago, she was left home alone with Elinor Neitzel, a young girl confined to bed with scarlet fever while her family was outside working the farm. In addition to feeling hot and achy, Elinor was lonely and bored in her dark room and hungry from not eating much for days. The old dog knew it, and she realized on some dog level that Elinor needed food to regain her strength and raise her spirits.

The dog went to the pantry and stole a loaf of bread, which, of course, she'd have liked nothing better than to have devoured right there on the spot. Seeming more concerned about Elinor than about herself, though, the dog carried the bread in her teeth to the little girl's pillow and nudged it toward her face, a beautiful gesture of understanding and sensitivity.

Then there is this story of an extraordinary rottweiler living in Panama City, Florida. Police picked him up on a street outside a bar at 2:30 A.M. with a five-year-old girl. The child had woken in the night and discovered that her mother had left her home alone—and had surely gone out drinking with her friends, as usual. Probably feeling totally abandoned, the child went outside and headed toward her mother's favorite bar.

When the police found the girl, they had no idea where she lived; and she couldn't tell them because she was disabled and could not speak. Deputy Sheriff Lee Heathcott and his German shepherd were called in to track the child's steps back to her house. Heathcott found that the girl had been wandering around for at least two-and-a-half hours through ditches, marshes, and woods. Shivering in the cool night air, she'd walked dark, empty streets and docks, where she could easily have fallen into the water and drowned.

The rottweiler, a former stray who surely understood how it felt to be cold and hungry, sensed the girl's vulnerability. "I could tell from the tracks that the dog was never more than a foot or two away from the child," says Heathcott. A better parent than the child's human mother, the dog, just five months old, never left the little girl for a minute. In his teeth, the sensitive dog carried her blanket.

I was moved by these stories but truly amazed by an account I heard of Lulu, an incredibly sensitive, 209-pound pig from Beaver Falls, Pennsylvania. Lulu looked like a giant, hairy mushroom with a thick gray hide and spindly legs, not exactly the picture of empathy. But then one day her guardian, Jo Ann Altsman, had a heart attack.

Jo Ann was home alone at the time. She lay, terrified, sprawled on the floor. She didn't think she could get up to dial 9-1-1; making any kind of physical effort in her condition could be even more life-threatening. Certain she was going to die alone with no one to help her, Jo Ann started to pray. In her mind, her whole life paraded before her, and she began to cry.

Then Lulu waddled over to Jo Ann and started crying, too. "Big fat tears were running down her snout and dripping off it," Jo Ann remembers. "The more I cried, the more she kept putting her head over me and making terrible sobbing sounds. She kept trying to kiss me."

Even though Jo Ann was so scared and upset, she was as concerned about Lulu as Lulu was about her. Jo Ann kept reassuring the pig, "Mommy's okay. You go night-night. Mommy's okay."

Instead of curling up and taking a nap, however, Lulu wriggled her huge body through a tiny door made for Jo Ann's twenty-five-pound dog, and the pig cut herself badly in the process. Bleeding all over the yard, she unlatched the front gate with her snout, then went to the street, where she threw herself, hooves up in the air, in front of passing cars. Most drivers, wanting nothing to do with a bleeding pig, made their way around her and did not stop to offer the help that Lulu was trying so hard to get for Jo Ann. Every few minutes, the pig would return through the dog door and cut herself worse each time.

"Lulu kept coming back to check on me to see if I was better or if she could help me," Jo Ann explains. On each visit the pig kept crying those big, fat, sensitive tears that comforted Jo Ann and made her feel that Lulu understood her desperation and cared about her. The caring pulled her through until a driver finally stopped for Lulu on the street and summoned an ambulance for Jo Ann.

We've seen how sensitive and attuned to us animals can be, and how that sensitivity prompts gestures meant to comfort us. The question is, what enables animals to be so perceptive about our situation and our needs?

For one thing, animals have emotions—deep, intense emotions that are like great puddles of feeling. Animals don't just occasionally feel things; they operate on a strong emotional level most of the time. During the course of just ten minutes, a dog can go from extreme joy—you're home!—to extreme sadness—no walk?—to extreme joy again—food! Animals' feelings rule their lives—and have everything to do with their choosing to do good.

Experts are beginning to acknowledge that animals do, in fact, feel anger, depression, anxiety, and joy. As University of Connecticut communication sciences and psychology professor Ross Buck puts it, "There is converging evidence that animals have emotions just like ours. They express emotions in the same way we do"—through posture, gesture, facial expression, body language, behavior, and vocalization. It is these emotions they themselves experience that allow animals to identify with what humans feel.

Part of the converging evidence has to do with brain anatomy. The limbic system, which is the part of the brain associated with emotion, looks just about the same in humans as it does in, say, pigs, like Lulu. Humans and most higher mammals receive similar emotional signals from their similar limbic systems. But our response to the signals differs from animals' because of the difference in the size of our brain's cortex, which is a large cauliflower-like mass that covers our limbic system. Its size varies according to species but is, generally, much larger in humans than in any other animal.

The cortex is the part of the brain where thinking and information processing take place. Since we have more cortical tissue, we have more computing power than do non-human species. The difference in cortex size also allows us to express our feelings in more complex ways. Says Temple Grandin, a Colorado State University professor who specializes in the humane treatment of farm animals, "A sad dog may whine. But when the raw emotions of the limbic system filter through the human's great big cortex, you get a Shakespearean sonnet to express the sadness."

Though emotional expression may vary, more converging evidence of the similarity between human and animal emotion can be seen through the study of brain chemistry. New brain scanning techniques have allowed us to see how brain chemicals, called neurotransmitters, carry messages from brain cell to brain cell. When specific neurotransmitters appear in people's brains, those individuals report that they are experiencing specific feelings. In this way we've learned, for instance, that the neurotransmitter dopamine is flooding our brain when we feel aroused. Endorphins are connected with a feeling of euphoria; seratonin with feelings of calmness and tranquillity. These same chemicals have been shown to appear in animals' brains. The logical conclusion is that the chemicals' presence in animals' brains indicates an experience of the same emotions described by humans.

It's also logical to conclude that animals have feelings similar to ours because they respond much as we do to the drugs we take for emotional problems. Stressed-out dogs stop panting, whining, and pacing when given the human anti-anxiety drug BuSpar. Nervous horses, confined to stalls, quit biting themselves when given Naltrexone, a drug prescribed to stop self-injuries in children. Birds, who are so agitated that they pluck out their feathers—just as people pluck out their hair with a disorder called trichotillomania—end the obsessive-compulsive behavior when they take Prozac, which, by elevating the brain's serotonin, brings calm and a sense of well-being to humans.

Animals may not be able to sit down and talk about their feelings of fear or depression, but they surely experience those emotions and empathize with them in us. As the old saying goes, "It takes one to know one," and it takes an animal who understands loneliness or anger to understand when we are having the same feelings. On a basic, limbic-system level, animals can feel what we are going through.

Ziggy, an eight-pound capuchin monkey, never fails to empathize with the feelings of Andrea Campbell, who has been raising her for the last ten years in Hot Springs Village, Arkansas.

Ziggy

Campbell works with Helping Hands, an organization that trains animals how to act as legs and arms for quadriplegics or otherwise disabled people. Campbell got Ziggy from Discovery Island in Walt Disney World when she was only five weeks old. Unable to hang on to her mother's abdomen, as baby monkeys do in the wild, Ziggy clung instead to Campbell's wrist. "For the first eight months she was like a furry Timex," says Campbell, author of *Bringing Up Ziggy*. While Campbell vacuumed, sewed buttons on her sons' shirts, or washed dishes, the monkey hung on and watched.

Because Ziggy witnessed all the emotional intricacies of Campbell's life, Campbell says the two are "so in tune with each other that she's like a little barometer of my feelings." Campbell signs e-mail messages "zigandme" to show there's no more emotional space between them than the space between words.

When Campbell cries, Ziggy cries. When Campbell gets mad, so does the monkey. During family spats, the hair on Ziggy's head stands straight up, like a buzz cut, bristling, as she raises her eyebrows, bares her teeth, and yells at whomever Campbell is reprimanding. "Ziggy plays my backup, like she's there to sing the chorus for the Supremes," Campbell says. " 'You did something out of line,' she's saying. 'We're gonna tell you what it is.' " Just as huffy as Campbell, Ziggy gets right into the argument.

Some people might see this sharing of feelings as a phenomenon called "emotional contagion," meaning that Ziggy gets vicariously aroused by what Campbell feels, that she "catches" Campbell's emotions just as people catch each other's colds. Indeed, Campbell's feelings may spread to Ziggy in that way, and the monkey may reflect them.

But more is going on when Ziggy freely chooses to stay open to Campbell's feelings and to show concern for her. It's most evident when Campbell gets depressed. After receiving a discouraging letter from an editor one afternoon, she sat down on the bed beside Ziggy and, with a heavy heart, felt certain that her writing career was over. "I just caved in," Campbell remembers. "I started bawling." Attuned to the despair, Ziggy hugged her, then went into a comforting mode. She climbed up to Campbell's shoulder, leaned lovingly against her, and groomed every hair on Campbell's head to console her. Says Campbell, "That's how Ziggy shows she cares."

Another reason animals may be so sensitive toward us is because they share some of our experiences. Though animals' lives are different from ours in many respects, we do exist on the planet together; and so we have much in common. Like us, animals burn themselves, choke on water, fall down, feel woozy and sick, are startled by loud noises. Animals experience hunger and pain and cold. They brace themselves against the attacks of bullies or the chills of bad weather or the cruelties of fate, just as we do. They find themselves alone sometimes, and feel isolated.

Cattle specialist Temple Grandin once told me that when animals experience something, it stays in their brain as a picture. Animals think in those pictures, she believes, rather than in our word-based, linear way. "Animals are able to make an association between what they are seeing in the present and a visual image stored in their memory," she explains. "When something's going on, [they] look for a similar situation that can serve as a model for how to respond."

A mental picture of a past experience can help animals understand what they perceive us going through, especially when we are in distress. Take, for example, the nearly universal experience of getting lost. Most animals probably have some kind of mental picture of being lost that enables them to remember the fear and loneliness of that situation. As a result, we see frequent newspaper accounts of dogs in particular who have shone with empathy upon finding a lost child.

In northwest Arkansas, on the banks of the Buffalo National River, Misty Hagar, age twelve, wandered away from her foster family on a winter afternoon. In the rugged terrain of cliffs and hills that look exactly alike, she got lost. As the temperature dropped to twenty degrees that night, a helicopter with infrared search equipment hovered over the area, and bloodhounds and a hundred-person search party combed the ground, with no luck.

Because a snowstorm was on its way and Misty was wearing only light pants and a jacket, searchers were scared that she would freeze to death. But they needn't have worried. Scotty, a mutt who looks like a dust mop, showed up out of nowhere and comforted and supported Misty. Even though he'd never seen the girl before, and his own well-heated home was not far away, Scotty kept her warm all night. He also hid Misty's tennis shoes, a curiously appropriate act that kept her from walking farther into the woods and getting more lost. Once searchers found the dog and the girl by the river the next morning, Scotty seemed to know he wasn't needed anymore and his comforting was done. He simply walked back home.

While Scotty wasn't lost, as Misty was, he may have understood from his own past experiences that she was vulnerable and needed help, and so he chose to stay with her. I've heard many other stories of animals getting into difficult situations *with* us and being just as frightened and distressed as we are. They can easily empathize with what we're going through because they're going through it, too. Yet even when they're also scared or in pain, the animals often still choose to be sensitive and to try to comfort us.

Buddy, for example, was a starving, abused stray, perhaps

one-part pit bull and one-part boxer. On a freezing December night, he was trying to keep warm in a tiny space between the floor and a well on a porch in Brown Summit, North Carolina. Mail carrier Kimberly Cheek didn't see him crouched there as she helped a man on her route carry groceries into his kitchen. And she also didn't see the well. Its flimsy plywood cover had slipped off, and she tripped and fell in. Says Cheek, "I grabbed anything I could get my hands on to keep from falling." What she grabbed was Buddy.

The two crashed thirty-five feet to the well's bottom. Screaming on her way down, Cheek scraped the skin off her back and shoulders on the rocks that lined the well. She ended up wedged sideways, her feet and ankles almost touching the back of her head, in nearly a foot of icy water. Buddy landed on top of her.

Cheek was terrified, not just because she might never get out of the well alive but also because, under beams of the flashlight her rescuers shone on her, Buddy looked like a purebred pit bull, a breed that had always sent chills of fear along Cheek's spine. Even the volunteer firemen who soon arrived were scared of the dog. While they lowered a blanket to Cheek, they tried to figure out how to get the dog up without being bitten. Buddy had to come up first because Cheek could not stand or move until they took him off her.

But, says Cheek, "Buddy knew we were both in a horrible, dangerous situation, and he was just as afraid as I was." His shivers from cold and fear were as violent and frequent as hers. "Knowing I was afraid," she adds, "he still tried to calm me." Under the blanket, Buddy nuzzled Cheek, lay his head against her neck, even stretched his own neck over to reach her shoulders, where he licked her wounds, she believes, to try to clean them. "He knew I was hurt," she says. He was sensitive. He cared.

The pitiful, bedraggled dog, who, as a stray, knew all about life's harshness, had no choice but to stay in the well with Kim. But even though he'd never seen her before, he also chose to "stay" with her emotionally, connect, and show concern. For two-and-a-half hours, until firemen harnessed him and pulled him up, then got Kim out, Buddy comforted her and kept her from panicking, she says. Her grateful husband, Andy, now points out that "dog is G-o-d spelled backward."

Animals, I am certain, bear their share of the world's cross with us. No matter how pampered their lives, they know firsthand about distress and suffering. In their own way and from their own hardships, they can identify with our own harsh times. Animals' difficult experiences, past or present, enable them to empathize with ours and to choose to comfort and be sensitive to us.

Shared emotions and experiences are not the only explanations of why animals can be so sensitive to us. There's also their ability to be incredibly observant. Animals *must* be observant. If they weren't, they'd be dead. Without reading subtle cues about others' feelings and physical conditions, animals could never mate, catch prey, protect themselves and their offspring from predators, or live together in a mutually beneficial social group. Their crucial highly developed observational powers lead to empathy.

This empathy is not necessarily innate. It has to be learned. Mother rhesus monkeys, for instance, teach empathy by carrying their babies around nonstop. In this way, the babies come to understand trust and emotional attachment. After three months, the mothers push away their babies to force them to play with their peers, and then the hard-core empathy lessons start. In rough-and-tumble games, young monkeys catch on all too quickly to other monkeys' signals of anger, fear, disgust, and sexual arousal. This crash course in observing and understanding nuances in others' feelings and behavior helps the monkeys get through life.

Most animals read subtleties in others far better than we can. Animals pick up gentleness in voices and anger in frowns as we do, but they also detect stress in salty-sweat smells and fear in rapid heartbeats. Not much gets by animals. Sometimes their power of observation is almost uncanny, especially when it comes to recognizing subtle signs of illness. Animals can choose to turn their gift of observation into sensitivity to us when we are sick.

Beetlejuice is a yellow-headed, orange-eared cockatiel. Darcy Ogburn brought him home as an orphaned, bald, four-week-old fledgling, weighing less than an ounce. For months, Darcy fed the bird crushed millet and formula from an eyedropper. Beetlejuice slept at night on Darcy's pillow and sat all day on his shoulder.

"We got close," admits Darcy, a tough and crusty ex-marine in Ormond Beach, Florida. "I had frequent conversations with this guy. He looked at me as if he understood."

How did Beetlejuice convey the understanding?

"His eye contact. Beetlejuice's eyes definitely had a lot of depth," Darcy explains. "He'd cock his head when I talked. He still bobs his head up and down to tell me 'yes.'"

Five years ago, Darcy was diagnosed with lymphoma. For weeks he lay on the sofa, "feeling sick and sorry for myself," he admits. Beetlejuice, who typically perched on Darcy's ankles, would march up his body to his chest, fluff up his feathers, and hunker down. Permanently.

In order to get the bird to eat, Darcy had to move Beetlejuice to his food and sit with him. If Darcy got up from the sofa for any reason, Beetlejuice was waiting there to hop back on his chest. "It was like he was on guard duty, like he was protecting me," Darcy says. "He understood that I felt bad, and he came to stand over me and comfort me. He thought that just being there would help me, and it did."

The amazing part of this empathy of bird for man is that today, Beetlejuice knows exactly when Darcy needs comforting. The bird cuddles up on his chest only when Darcy is really sick; forget it if he has a cold. Darcy believes that Beetlejuice can tell serious illness from malingering through his feet—by feeling Darcy's heart beat faster or harder from pain and anxiety on his sickest days.

That may be right. According to Sally Blanchard, a parrot behaviorist in Alameda, California, parrots have bundles of en-capsulated nerve endings, called Herbst's corpuscles, on their knees and feet. These nerve endings allow the birds to detect vi-brations, such as predators sneaking down a tree limb toward them. Beetlejuice might well use his feet for sensitively evaluating Darcy's condition.

As far as turning that sensitivity into empathy, Blanchard says, "Parrots pick up your energy and have a gut level, immedi-ate reaction to what's going on." Their effort to comfort can be explained because "birds love us," she adds. All Darcy's love and care for Beetlejuice as a fledgling may be coming back to him like a boomerang.

Sometimes animals can get so attached and sensitive to us that the animals are able to sense that we are sick even before we know it. Dogs and cats have been known to warn people that they have cancer or are about to have a migraine or a medical emergency. One of those dogs is Dakota, a golden retriever from Dallas, Texas.

Dakota was a service dog, whom a doctor "prescribed" for

Mike Lingenfelter as a way to help him recover from depression and anxiety. The dog soon boosted Lingenfelter's morale so much that they started going together to schools, where Lingenfelter would give talks about pet care while Dakota sat quietly at his feet.

On one such visit, though, the dog suddenly whined, paced, and poked his nose against his guardian's leg with great agitation. Says Lingenfelter, "I was embarrassed because I'd just been talking with the students about how service dogs are so well behaved." Dakota started barking, and Lingenfelter led him out of the classroom. Once out in the hall, Lingenfelter, who had a chronic heart condition, sank to the floor with a heart attack.

Over the next few months, there were several occasions in which Dakota would act exactly as he had that day, just moments before Lingenfelter would develop angina pains. Finally, Lingenfelter figured out that the dog was sensing changes in the smell of his sweat, caused by a release of enzymes when his heart began malfunctioning.

And Dakota's sensitivity was not limited to picking up cues about his guardian's physical condition. Lingenfelter later took the dog to his office, where Dakota rushed down the hall to a colleague's office—and whined and barked. A few minutes later, the man had a heart attack. Dakota had wanted him to know that it was coming.

Percy, a St. Bernard, regularly predicts the seizures of Melanie Horne, a diabetic in Seattle. Horne brought Percy home as a puppy and worked for months to train him to pull her wheelchair, open the front door and refrigerator, and bring her juice or the telephone. Somewhere along the line, Percy developed what Horne calls "an extraordinary sense of responsibility." He also seems to have acquired an ability to smell changes in her blood sugar levels, or hear her heartbeats slow, or note tiny shifts in her mood, facial expression, and behavior—all subtle signals that may tell him that Horne is about to lose consciousness.

One afternoon last year, Percy padded up to Horne on his huge paws, stared in her face, and whined. Since he always behaved this way to warn her that she was in trouble, Horne got out her glucometer and tested her blood sugar. Percy had been right: It was dropping very quickly. Knowing she had little time before blacking out, Horne managed to say, "Get the phone." The dog brought it to her. She punched 9-1-1 and mumbled something about being diabetic. And that's all she remembers.

When she opened her eyes, Horne had a blood-pressure cuff around her arm and a paramedic was leaning over her. Percy, with his tail wagging, had opened the front door and ushered the ambulance team to Horne in the living room. Then he'd moved out of the way while the paramedics gave her a glucose injection. Without his sensitivity to her, she might have died that afternoon—in a heap on the floor.

When Horne regained consciousness, she was lying on the sofa. But the paramedics had not brought her there. Percy had dragged her, unconscious, to the house's softest place, where he himself always liked to lounge. With an uncanny understanding of her illness *and* her need for comfort, he had chosen to be sensitive to both.

Animals' power of observation allows them to pick up subtle signals of not just our physical, but also our emotional state. I once had a psychology professor who told me that he encouraged clients in his marriage-and-family-counseling practice to bring their dogs to therapy sessions. He could see, he said, who was in the most emotional pain by what family member the dog chose to sit by. The dog selected whoever needed comfort most.

Plywood, a plywood-colored Labrador retriever in Pound Ridge, New York, was the epitome of sensitivity in this respect.

A stray until Marty Rosenblum took him in, the dog still often roamed the neighborhood. He appeared one day at the home of Jim Dunn, who had terminal cancer and must surely have been dealing with anxiety, despair, and endless questions of "why me?"

As Dunn gradually got sicker, Plywood would return every single day, even in rain and snow. He was polite about the visits, too. He showed up in the mornings, left around four o'clock, and never went nosing about through the house.

All that changed on the day Dunn died. Plywood somehow knew that Dunn had only a short time left. Locked in his own house, the dog was so determined to get to Dunn that he pushed his way through a screen door. He ran to Dunn's house and walked straight into the bedroom, where he lay his head on Dunn's arm and sat with him for hours.

For months Plywood's presence had made Dunn feel needed and secure. The dog distracted him from feelings of worry and anxiety and helped him cope with his sense of isolation and despair. Plywood had been so important to Dunn, in fact, that his family put a photo of the dog into the casket.

Observant and sensitive animals, like Plywood, can choose to help us die in peace. Animals' ability to comfort us can also help us heal.

At the University of Pennsylvania years ago, Aaron Katcher and Erica Friedman proved that living with a pet increases your chance of surviving for a year after a heart attack. Petting an animal you are bonded to, they found, can lower your heart rate and your skin's conductivity of minute electric currents, which indicates that you're sweating less from anxiety. In research at Cambridge University, James Serpell discovered that people who brought a dog into their homes benefited from a better sense of security and self-esteem and suffered less from headaches, cold, and flu. In a recent study of forty-eight stockbrokers on blood pressure medication, Karen Allen and Joseph Izzo, at the State

Spooky with Judge David Breck

University of New York at Buffalo, found that the subjects who took in a pet reduced by fifty percent their stress-related rise in blood pressure.

Some Tokyo companies have been paying $4,000 a month to a firm, called Pet Plan 110, to bring a dog, cat, or pig to their offices each day to ease tensions. Michigan Judge David Breck regularly takes Spooky, "the prettiest and smartest cat in the world," he says, to his court chambers. Spooky interrupts his naps to sidle up to hostile attorneys, and he rubs against their ankles. Says Breck, "The lawyers' antagonism seems to diminish. If

they can be more open and relaxed, then cases get settled easier." He figures that Spooky "de-spooks" about 2,000 lawyers annually by making the chambers more homey and less threatening.

The mere presence of some sensitive animals can make us feel better. So can their specific attributes that underscore the sensitivity. Animals have three of the qualities that famous psychologist Carl Rogers said were crucial for counselors: empathy, unconditional positive regard, and congruence, meaning being truly who they are without pretense. Perhaps congruence is involuntary; animals, who are so natural, are not necessarily adept at artifice. On the other hand, they certainly *choose* whether to empathize and accept us positively, no strings attached. That choice makes all the difference in how readily animals can heal us; and the healing is all the greater when we feel that animals come to us because they are sensitive to our emotions or our circumstances.

Janet Ruckert, a Los Angeles psychologist and author of *The Four-Footed Therapist*, discovered by accident just how easily sensitive animals can heal, when she brought her Burmese cat, Clancy, to her office before a veterinary appointment. Clancy came over to Ruckert's client, a little girl, and curled up, purring, in her lap. For the first time the child opened up and talked about her parents' divorce. "The interaction between the cat and the child was startling," says Ruckert. So startling that she brought in her rottweilers, Cachet and Alix, who walked up to clients, wagged their tails, and were totally uninhibited about showing how much they liked each person. That freely given, positive welcome made clients feel accepted, Ruckert realized, just as touching the dogs' fur made them feel tranquil and safe. Steps toward healing, to be sure.

When animals approach us and eagerly allow us to hug them, they can become what psychologists call "transitional objects." Those objects are parent substitutes, the things we hold on to for the same security and love that we were supposed to have gotten from our mothers and fathers, the very first "objects" we attach ourselves to for warmth and safety after birth. Stuffed animals and Linus's blanket serve as transitional objects. Live animals can be even better—and more healing—especially when they volunteer, like small, attentive mothers and fathers, to accept us unconditionally and show they empathize and care.

Two cats, Paddy and Pixie, did this for their guardian Anne Williams in Lawrenceville, New Jersey, when she was grieving the death of her mother. Instead of choosing to go out their always-open cat door and prowl the neighborhood, they showed up in Williams's bed each night between exactly 2:00 and 3:00 A.M.

That was "the critical hour," she says, the time when her mother had died and Williams was most likely to be lying awake in the dark, fighting loneliness and sorrow. For *two years*, until Williams worked through her loss, the sensitive cats picked up her emotions and arrived at that specific time, she believes, in order to comfort her. Until morning, Paddy and Pixie would radiate warmth and security, like living, healing teddy bears.

A sensitive chicken named Sonya did the same for Karen Davis, founder of the animal rights organization United Poultry Concerns, in Machipongo, Virginia. Davis's great passion is farm birds; stopping their suffering is the meaning of her life. On the day that her favorite rooster was killed, she came home crying. Sonya walked over and buried her head in Davis's neck. "Sonya purred a little trilling sound, the way chickens do to comfort others," she says. "Her voice and behavior indicated clearly that she understood how sad I was, and her sensitivity and warmth made me feel so much better."

Animals also heal us by choosing to let us know in no uncertain terms just what *they're* feeling. In research, Ross Buck has found that showing your emotions is the most important part of empathy. "If you're expressive yourself, you carry that expressiveness *with* you," Buck explains. "And in response to it, others will be expressive *to* you."

In other words, by being open and honest about your emotions, you draw them out of others—and that promotes understanding, connectedness, and well-being. Animals show their feelings constantly; they are totally expressive. Sonya's soft trills and Paddy and Pixie's nightly arrival at the critical hour spoke volumes about their feelings of closeness and concern.

My favorite emotionally expressive—and healing—dog is Jessie, a supremely sensitive Labrador retriever from San Leandro, California. Jessie was totally devoted to Beverly Herrera, to whom she had been given as a puppy for her birthday. That connection explains the dog's great distress at being made to stay at the back of Beverly's truck while Beverly rode with her husband, Rudy, in the cab.

Rudy was adamant that the dog ride there, and only once did Jessie break the "don't-go-through-the-window" rule and climb into the cab. He got so mad that he pulled the truck over and bodily forced her back through the window. "He gave her the scolding of her life," Beverly remembers. "Her feelings were terribly hurt."

Jessie learned her lesson, but everything changed on a terrible night when Beverly and Rudy were camping with Jessie and Muffin, their thirteen-year-old, blind, and very sickly cat. Muffin began gasping for breath. Beverly and Rudy put Jessie in the back of the truck and rushed the cat to the emergency clinic. En route Muffin's heart stopped beating, and her tongue turned gray. Just as Beverly handed Muffin to the clinic's vet technician, the cat died. Inconsolable, Beverly returned, crying, to the truck.

She heard movement behind her. When she and Rudy turned around, Jessie had one foot tentatively inside the window to the cab. "She was looking at me with the saddest eyes I've ever seen," Beverly says. "Jessie turned to Rudy with an expression that seemed to insist, 'I don't care what you do to me, but I'm going to Beverly. She needs me.' "

Jessie wriggled through the window, and Rudy didn't say a word. Pressing her body against Beverly, the dog rested her chin on Beverly's shoulder. Crying uncontrollably, Beverly held on to Jessie like a lifeline. The dog just stayed there, quiet and warm and sensitive, her close presence expressing, better than words, that she understood Beverly's sadness and was eager to console her.

When Beverly calmed down, she mumbled, "Thank you, Jessie."

As if on cue, the dog seemed to know that her healing comforting had done its job. "Jessie quietly turned around and climbed back through the window into the back of the truck," Beverly remembers. "She never went through the window again."

Some researchers say that animals, like Jessie, come to us when we're sick or upset only because they want to be fussed over and petted, or because they are confused. An animal behaviorist once explained to me that when animals see us crying or lying sick in bed, they don't understand the strange behavior; so they lie down submissively beside us to ask our permission to let them try and figure out why we're acting so oddly.

Don't you believe it. Animals don't come to us just to get our attention or reassurance. There are too many examples of animals being sensitive just because that's the way they choose to be. One is Moxie, a buckskin quarter horse, whose impeccable attentiveness was a great help to Kacey Ruegsegger after she was wounded in the 1999 shootings at Columbine High School.

Hiding under a computer table, Kacey was plugging her ears with her fingers to muffle the noise of the gunshots when a bullet hit the back of her shoulder, went through her right hand, across her throat, and into her left hand. The bones in her shoulder, upper arm, and right hand were shattered.

Before these debilitating injuries, Kacey had been trying hard to qualify for the American Quarter Horse World Youth Show. Every day after school and on weekends, she'd worked with Moxie, and all the work had paid off. She'd gotten more points than any contestant in Colorado to qualify for three of the World Youth Show's events.

One bullet shattered Kacey's dream, just like her bones. Doctors told her, "It's too risky for you to ride. If you got dumped off your horse, your bones would break again."

When Kacey went home from the hospital, still weak and with her arm and hand in an awkward splint, she insisted on seeing Moxie before she'd take one step into the house. Her parents were nervous because Moxie had always been a very frisky horse—"a pistol," in the words of her mother, Darcy.

But the eleven-hundred-pound animal was instantly sensitive to Kacey. Darcy describes how Moxie took one look at her and understood that she was hurt. "There was a whole different demeanor about him. His eyes looked really worried. He put his ears forward and made a purposeful, gentle act of nuzzling Kacey's bandaged arm, almost as if to say, 'I know something's wrong.' He really knew he had to be careful because there was a problem with her and she wasn't the same."

Kacey hung around the barn every chance she got, talked to Moxie, and brushed him with her less badly hurt left hand. Between constant appointments with doctors and physical therapists, Kacey wondered if she and Moxie could at least enter the showmanship competition, which required her only to walk along with him in a pattern.

Her surgeon was firmly opposed until, finally, Kacey demonstrated just how she would lead Moxie by the reins. "Okay," he relented, "but you have to promise if the horse pulls you, you'll let go. You can't put yourself at risk."

Because of her bandages, Kacey had to lead Moxie with the wrong hand, but the horse willingly changed his usual way of doing things to accommodate her injury. At the show, Kacey and

Moxie won the competition, and the audience sprang, applauding, to their feet. A month later Kacey had healed so well that her surgeon finally allowed her to ride. When Kacey first mounted Moxie, he didn't prance and buck, as he'd often done before. "He was careful about how he moved his body," Darcy remembers. "He was quiet and gentle."

Kacey's long absence from competition had stopped her from accumulating points to qualify for the American Quarter Horse World Youth Show. But that didn't keep her and Moxie from entering other events. They won the all-around competition in a Colorado show, then almost made the finals at another in Ohio.

"The bond between Kacey and Moxie gave her the will to get well," Darcy believes. "Moxie chose to help her get back to where she needed to be. The love of that animal helped heal her"—body *and* soul.

Moxie, as do so many animals, chose to be sensitive. When we are unhappy, depressed, or anxious, animals can feel what we're feeling and go through it right along with us. Says social scientist Margot Lasher, "that connection heals us and comforts us. With animals, we're not alone."

2.

COMPASSION

L et me tell you about Heart and Soul.

Heart was an abandoned mutt, a great white ball of fluff who surely had a Samoyed ancestor tucked somewhere in the leaves of his family tree. A forest ranger spotted him and summoned Leo Grillo, founder of Dedication and Everlasting Love to Animals (D.E.L.T.A. Rescue) in Glendale, California.

"There's a dog over there." The ranger pointed down the road. "Looks like he's dying."

Grillo found Heart behind a log near a pond, where coyote packs usually denned in the reeds. Muddy and sodden as a wet sponge, he was curled up in a puddle of rainwater where he had dragged himself to cool his wounds. "He looked like someone had taken a knife and

Heart

slashed him to ribbons," Grillo remembers. The dog was listless and barely breathing, in shock not just from excruciating pain, but also from loss of blood.

Huddled next to Heart was his three-month-old daughter, Soul. Below her ears were Heart's same fluffy sideburns. Her sweet face and dark, sad eyes were identical to his, only smaller and more delicate.

At D.E.L.T.A. Rescue's hospital, the vet found that Heart's abdomen and rear legs were shredded. His chest and neck had puncture wounds from teeth. Grillo knew exactly what had happened to the dog, and his theory was confirmed a few days later at the pond, where Grillo found paw prints in the mud, now dried to a crust—prints that showed chaos, frenzied motion, and terror.

Heart and Soul had been dumped in the wilderness, Grillo figured. They'd walked for miles to find a warm, dry hiding place and food. As they searched, they'd met a coyote pack, just as eager for a meal. Tiny Soul was, as Grillo puts it, "a perfect coyote supper." Reading the paw prints like the words in a book, Grillo concluded that the hungry coyotes circled the father and daughter and got ready to kill.

But Heart probably lured the coyotes away to give Soul the chance to run and hide. As the coyotes cut off Heart's escape, the fight began in earnest; and he defended his daughter with every bit of strength he had. The dog won, and the coyotes ran away. Heart dragged himself to the ditch behind the log, where Soul came and curled up beside him.

In the hospital Grillo left Heart's cage door open, so Soul could stay close to him. For days she lay on the floor and lifted her head up to rest next to his inside the cage. Whenever he woke, she licked his face as if she were trying to encourage him and tell him that he'd been the world's greatest father. Soul

Soul visits Heart in the hospital

seemed to take great care not to brush against Heart's sutures and cause him pain.

It doesn't take much to imagine the deep, powerful emotions between Heart and Soul or a father's absolute determination to save his daughter. He must have seen the coyotes and, with both terror and rage, known that he would fight to the death to protect her. As teeth ripped into him, Heart must have wanted to run and hide and save himself, but he didn't. He took the pain, so Soul would be spared.

Says Grillo, "Animals care desperately about each other." He should know: With fourteen hundred animals at his sanctuary, Grillo sees creatures, like Heart and Soul, show their desperate caring every day through acts of kindness to each other.

Scientists generally don't refer to animals as being "kind" because they find it too close to the anthropomorphism that they steer away from in their professional world. Instead, scientists tend to discuss behavior like Heart's in terms of possible animal "altruism." They define it as an animal helping another at a cost to itself without getting anything in return.

I go deeper with my own definition and add emotion. To me, altruism—or kindness or compassion—starts with the sensitivity we saw in the last chapter. Animals understand another's situation, and often they try to offer comfort or support, both of which, of course, have kindness in them. But so often animals choose to do more than just be sensitive. They dive in and act in sometimes amazing and dramatic ways to solve whatever problem another may be having. The action, which is often absolutely selfless, turns the empathy into kindness. Compassion, in fact, is empathy in action.

All species of animals can choose to be compassionate. In a study led by Jules Masserman in Northwestern University's neurology and psychiatry department, fifteen rhesus monkeys were taught to pull two chains for a pellet of food. On the fourth day of the experiment, one of the chains was also cruelly programmed to give an electric shock to another monkey a short distance away. After witnessing the monkey being shocked and seeing its distress, a majority of the others refused to pull the chain even to get the food. One wouldn't pull *either* chain for five days and another, for twelve—even if their reluctance meant hunger. The study's researchers labeled the monkeys' behavior "protective" and "altruistic."

In a study reported in *Animal Behavior Abstracts*, French researchers found that rats could also behave with altruism. The researchers gave rats a drink of an unpleasantly salty lithium chloride solution. When other rats were put in the cage with the original group, those who had already sampled the unsavory liquid pushed the others away from it. The rats seemed to be looking out for the newcomers' well-being and trying to spare them a lousy drink. It seems even rodents can be kind.

It may be easier to imagine kindness in monkeys and rats, fellow mammals, than in fish, whom we tend to view as cold in blood *and* in deed. Yet, as Austin Lamberts, a neurosurgeon in Grand Rapids, Michigan, discovered, even fish can show compassion. In an informal experiment, he put a fish in a bowl containing a five-percent solution of ethyl alcohol. When the fish got drunk, Lamberts scooped it back into a tank with nine others. For sixteen days, he alternated which fish got the alcohol. He found that when a fish was intoxicated, the others would take care of it. One always stayed close by and guarded the drunk fish until it sobered up and could swim straight.

There is no doubt in my mind that compassion among *all* animal species goes on around us constantly, all over the planet, at every hour of the day and night. The kindness can be a small, sometimes inconvenient favor, such as a zebra nibbling ticks off another zebra's neck. Or it can be a life-threatening sacrifice, like Heart's. Whether subtle or dramatic, the compassion is there. All we have to do is open our eyes and see it.

But many scientists seem to be in a quandary about whether animal altruism exists. Some researchers argue that animals are incapable of understanding others' needs and that self-interest lies beneath what might look like kindness. The self-interest, which is sometimes blatant, sometimes subtle, they insist, is always lurking in the shadows—and it keeps animals' behavior from ever qualifying as true altruism.

Several years ago Gerald Wilkinson, who teaches zoology at the University of Maryland, told me, "To my knowledge there is no convincing example in animals where altruism occurs."

What about Heart's heroic fight for Soul?

"An action may *look* altruistic," Wilkinson said. "But when you see who is doing what to whom or what time frame it happens in, then it's often possible to come up with an explanation that shows some sort of benefit to the individual who performs the act."

Supposedly, the benefit negates the animal altruism, and, under close scrutiny, animals turn out in the end always to get some benefit—and to choose their own needs over the needs of others. Wilkinson would explain Heart's action in terms of a scientific theory called kin selection. According to this view, animals who look like they're choosing to be kind to others are really just assisting their own relatives. They benefit in doing so by spreading copies of their own genes. By helping family, the theory goes, animals can ensure their species' survival and the continuation of their genes in the great progression of evolution. Genes are all that count.

Honeybees, supposedly driven by kin selection, sting predators and die to protect sisters, carrying their genes, in the hive. Female seagulls are said to care for the offspring of a male who's just lost his mate in order to pave the way for mating with him in the next season and promoting their own genes. Parents of all species presumably tend their biological babies in order to ensure that their genes will not die out.

These examples, of course, don't take into account animals' emotion, the love and caring that fuel compassion. Nor do the examples explain the undeniable passion that can lie behind animals' efforts to help their family members. With one swoop of a theory, there goes the devotion of Honey, a pathetic, stray Walker hound, who was brought to the attention of Pets Inc. in West Columbia, South Carolina.

I'm not sure who would dare claim that Honey, with love and concern for her pups practically bristling from her, was just a gene-driven mother. So scrawny that her ribs stuck out like 3-D stripes on her dingy fur, she was seen limping around a subdivision in 28-degree weather with a five-pound, double-spring, rusty metal trap, big enough to catch a bear, clamped to her foot. Attached to the trap was a long metal stake that had anchored the trap to the ground. Honey had chewed almost through her foreleg to free herself. When that hadn't worked, she tugged loose the whole trap and stake and hobbled off in agony.

Dave Johnston, the Pets Inc. rescuer who picked her up, discovered that her paw was almost gone; all that was left of it was a piece of pad and one claw, dangling. Bones protruded through her skin at the spot where she had chewed her leg. She was dutifully tending two puppies, though; and when Johnston put her and the pups in his truck, he says, "Her eyes were just looking at me, telling me, 'Thank you, thank you.' " He was sure the thanks were meant for rescuing not just her, but her puppies, too.

The pups explain why—after food and a trip to the vet, who bandaged her wounds—Honey kept limping painfully for hours, back and forth from the front door to the rear door at Pets Inc. The staff finally realized that she was frantic to get outside to other pups that hadn't yet been rescued. Dave Johnston found three more and reunited Honey with her family of five.

There was no doubt to anyone how much she cared about her babies. She licked them, nuzzled them, and showed what looked like love and kindness worthy of the *Guinness Book of Records*. "Honey would have died stuck in that trap if she hadn't wanted so badly to get back to her pups," says Pets Inc. co-founder Pat McQueen. In the bone-chilling winter weather, the dog had managed to keep the puppies reasonably healthy though nursing had turned her into skin and bones. Her sacrifice was surely driven by far more than gene preservation, as would have been a human mother's desperate efforts to save her children in a comparable situation. Honey's behavior was all about love and compassion.

And what about kin selection in the case of two horses, Yohanna and Shammy? "They're plain old common Kansas horses, grade mares," says Herb Bolyard, who keeps them on his ten-acre ranch outside Topeka, Kansas. Sisters born a year apart, they grew up together, grazed together, and were rarely out of each other's sight. If separated, they would whinny with great urgency to find each other. Their mutual devotion was what tipped off Bolyard that something was wrong when Yohanna, all alone and whinnying nonstop, ran up and down the fence next to the house one morning.

"I knew she was trying to get my attention," Bolyard says. He was certain that Shammy had broken out of the fence or was lying, stuck, somewhere, and that Yohanna wanted him to come and help.

Yohanna followed him like a shadow as he searched the farm on foot. When he couldn't find Shammy, he went to the barn for his truck, and Yohanna came, too. Just before he climbed behind the steering wheel, Bolyard glanced down at the pond and saw what looked like a piece of wood on the iced-over surface. Suddenly the wood began to move. "That's Shammy's head!" Bolyard shouted, apprehension stabbing him. "My God, she's fallen through the ice."

Shammy was floating in ten feet of water. The cold must have hit her like a train and left her reeling and shivering, then numb. As terror gripped her, she must have thrashed around to save herself. Now, exhausted, she could barely keep her head above the surface. Yohanna clearly understood her sister's danger and desperately wanted to help her.

As Bolyard ran to Shammy, Yohanna followed and stood beside the pond, anxiously watching every move he made to save her sister. Sometimes Yohanna walked around the bank to get a better view as firemen laid ladders on the ice and put a rope around Shammy's neck to pull her out. When that didn't work they used axes to chop a path through the ice to shore, and then led Shammy through the narrow, hastily constructed canal. Though she was so weak and cold that she could barely walk, she kept whinnying to Yohanna, and Yohanna kept whinnying back.

Yohanna's support may have been all that kept Shammy going as Bolyard and the firemen had to hook her to a cable and winch her to get her into the barn. Then they spent hours warming her. For every one of those hours, Yohanna, left outside to keep her out of the way, stood beside the closed barn door and waited, pawing her hooves into the dirt, turning in circles, and neighing. "She made her presence known to her sister," Bolyard says.

Chewing your leg to the bone so you can watch after your babies. Standing guard in the snow all day to encourage your sister. Those acts require intense concern and sacrifice. To me, they are vivid displays of compassion. To say that Honey and Yohanna were driven to spread copies of their genes seems coldly academic, an odd and inappropriate explanation for these dramas of kindness and love.

E volutionary biologists' other explanations for what looks like animal compassion have names like reciprocal altruism, pseudo-altruism, and by-product mutualism. Basically, all the theories boil down to one conclusion: Animals give just to get a payback. Depending on the theory, the payback can be direct or indirect, immediate or in the future. But it's always there, supposedly. And just as with kin selection, the payback turns animal kindness into ashes of self-interest.

Zoologist Gerald Wilkinson found vampire bats in Costa Rica that would feed colony members to whom they weren't related by regurgitating blood into their mouths at night. His explanation: The bats were feeding colony mates who'd had bad hunting luck, so they themselves would get a meal, tit-for-tat, when they came home hungry in the future. Providing blood for each other had nothing to do with true altruism, Wilkinson concluded; it was rather a reciprocal exchange of favors for the sake of brute survival. Bats fail to find blood about ten percent of the time they go out hunting; and if that happens two nights in a row, they die.

West German researcher O. Anne Rasa found that dwarf mongooses and hornbills wait for each other to show up before going out in the Taru Desert to forage for similar prey. The association, she decided, was based on fear of the same raptors that go after both mongooses and hornbills. The two species warn each other—from the different perspectives of ground and tree—and, thereby, increase their chances of not being snatched away by claws. This is mutualism; what might seem like altruism between species presumably amounts to mongooses and hornbills really getting simultaneous paybacks for being each other's sentinels. If they didn't help each other, they could quickly pay the price of death.

According to evolutionary biologists, when a lion nurses another female's cubs, she is not trying to help out a friend but rather is selfishly ensuring that her own cubs will have playmates, since male lions are said to reproduce better if they have male companions. Evening bats presumably nurse each other's pups for a different benefit: The mother is just dumping her milk so she'll weigh less when she goes hunting and can fly more easily and energetically. She also tends to nurse only female babies because females return to the colony but males don't; helping females supposedly means a larger future colony with more bats to find good foraging and roosting sites. No kindness there, it seems.

In examples like these, exchanging favors may have survival value. Altruism can pay off for animals, just as it does for humans. Nevertheless, it shouldn't be said that animals are always looking out for their own needs. For all the cases of animals who *may* give just to get, there are other stories of animals seeming to be kind in the truest sense and not seeking to get anything back by extending themselves.

In a University of Wisconsin study, for example, biologist Millicent Flicken found that a chickadee will let the rest of the flock know immediately when it has discovered a good source of food. Because chickadees will constantly join and leave a flock, this bird could not expect the others to repay the kindness. A flock's membership never stays the same for long, so there's no benefit for an individual bird to show compassion, Flicken concluded.

Marjorie Vallerga and her husband, Ed, bought a German shepherd puppy named Gus to be a companion for Thor, their elderly dog. At age thirteen, Thor had been moping around, his distinguished white muzzle on the floor, depressed after the death of the family's golden retriever.

All that changed when Gus arrived at the Vallergas' home in Paradise, California. He seemed to give Thor a new will to live. As a mentor to Gus, Thor shepherded him around the family's three acres, showed him the fence line, taught him the best spots to lie in the sun on lazy afternoons. But after a few months, Thor's age started catching up with him again. He seemed, wearily, to be slipping away.

One night Gus ran, barking, to Marj and Ed's bed. He pawed and whined and nudged them with his nose.

"Lie down. Go to sleep," Ed ordered him.

Wasted breath. Gus continued yapping.

He ran to the front door, then to the sliding glass door, left open each night so that he and Thor could get out for midnight expeditions. As Marj and Ed tried unsuccessfully to go back to sleep, Gus ran again to the front door, back to their bed, back to the dog door. Clearly he was making a statement, and he was urgent about it.

Finally, Marj and Ed got up and followed Gus down their front stairs and outside. There stood Thor, so arthritic and weak that he couldn't make it back up on his own into the house. As Marj and Ed looped towels under Thor's belly to support him and help him up the stairs, Gus, still a lively puppy who was always underfoot, backed up and carefully stayed out of the way.

"Gus knew Thor needed to be inside, and he needed help. And Gus knew he could come to us for it," said Marj.

What could an ancient, tired dog possibly have to offer a puppy, I wondered. "Did Gus have anything to gain from watching after Thor?" I asked.

"No. What Gus did was just true heart," Marj said. "Thor was Gus's friend and teacher. It was all an act of love, I'm sure."

For the next few days Gus's compassion took another form. As Thor became weaker, he lay in a worn-out heap on the living room floor. Gus seemed to know that Thor's life was draining out of him and that he needed peace and quiet. Controlling all his puppy energy, Gus stayed, silent and close, right next to his friend, only rarely leaving his side. Again with nothing to gain from being kind to an old, decrepit dog, Gus saw Thor through until the end.

Choosing to help others with no payback is a key to animal compassion, whether it's trying to find a way to get an old dog up some stairs or simply offering assistance to another who's having hard times. Vintage, a tiny, white barn cat, was the Olympic champion of assistance-giving. When it comes to showing kindness with no chance of getting something in return, her small and eager heart was whale-sized.

Vintage showed up, feral and emaciated, at the farm of Judy Rott, just outside Jamestown, North Dakota. Rott fed her and let her visit her chocolate Lab, Molly McTrouble, in a kennel near the barn. Like Thor and Gus, Vintage and Molly became inseparable. At night they slept snuggled up together, and during the day Molly would pick up the five-pound cat in her mouth and carry her from place to place. "A lot of trust and love developed between the two of them," Rott says. "I don't think they knew they were a different species. It was like they belonged together."

During one exceptionally hot and humid summer, both cat and dog got pregnant, and their babies arrived at the same time. Vintage went off by herself and gave birth, but her kittens were stillborn or killed—Rott isn't sure which. Molly, on the other hand, had nine lusty, yowling puppies in a whelping box in the garage. Though Molly nursed her babies endlessly, she only had eight teats for her nine pups. One was always hungry.

Vintage showed up at the garage and cried pitifully to be let in with her friend. But Rott, afraid the feral cat might give the puppies a disease, shooed her away. Vintage was persistent, though, and kept hanging around, meowing. Then one afternoon when Rott let Molly outside for a break, Vintage squeezed through the slightly open door and sneaked across the garage. She jumped into the box, and that was that.

Rott found Vintage nursing the puppies and licking them clean. She kept up this kindness for weeks. The babies grew so fond of the cat that Rott once tried to pick her up, and four of the pups hung on to her teats, as if the pups were attached by Velcro. Their constant, voracious, and indelicate sucking eventually stripped all the fur off Vintage's belly. Yet in spite of growing increasingly bald and thin, she refused to leave them or Molly.

Vintage had milk—and kindness—to give, and she gave it. Nonstop. At a great physical sacrifice. The question is whether she was getting a payback that made her compassionate behavior just an act of selfishness. Some experts have told me that Vintage nursed only to stop her swollen, milk-filled breasts from aching or, like a little automaton, to act out her maternal instinct, no matter the progeny. Rott disagrees: "I think Vintage cared. The cat wanted to help. She just had it in her to be kind."

I have collected a fat, overstuffed file of stories about animals choosing to show compassion to total strangers. Usually members of another species, these strangers aren't biological relatives. So no one can claim kin selection as an explanation for their behavior. The strangers are unknowns; the animals have never laid eyes on them before and, therefore, have no idea how the strangers might benefit them. So no one can claim that the kindness is extended just for a payback.

One of the most common ways that animals show compassion to strangers is by getting help for them if they're in trouble. A cat once led a woman to some pit bull pups that had fallen twelve feet into a crack in the earth in Hawaii. A Canadian horse stood guard over an injured baby rabbit and refused to leave until the tiny creature was rescued. More dogs than I can even count have led people to other dogs whom they don't know—trapped in storm drains, hanging upside down from fences, buried in snow, drowning in wells.

A dog in Arizona barked for help to save a turtle, flailing its legs in a desperate attempt to climb out of a swimming pool. Willy, a Labrador retriever in Illinois, barked for an hour in the snow to tell the world that a woman he'd never met before had fallen into the Des Plaines River. Chief, a big black, floppy-eared mutt did the same for a stranger buried up to his shoulders in snow in California. When his guardian, Bob Sollima, went to see what Chief was barking at, he found "this guy hanging on to my dog for dear life," he says. Besides calling for help, Chief had moved close to the man and let him grab on, so he wouldn't sink over his head in the snow.

Trouble, a St. Bernard, stands five-foot-ten on his hind paws and lumbers through life at a whopping 161 pounds. One day a woman screamed for help behind his house, but, as Trouble's owner, Dawn, says of their tough Louisville, Ohio, neighborhood, "Around here, you mind your own business, so I ignored the yells." She also ignored a gunshot.

Trouble didn't. When Dawn opened the door and called the dog inside, he turned around instead and jumped over their five-foot wooden gate, something he'd never done before. Barking ferocious, deep-chested barks, he charged to the middle of the street and ran off three men, who had just robbed, raped, and shot a woman visiting the neighborhood.

Then Trouble's viciousness changed to solicitude. He sat next to the woman, licked her bruised and swollen face, and kept her conscious until the ambulance came, at which time he tried to protect her from the paramedics—until Dawn came down and led him away, paws dragging with reluctance. She says, "He risked his own life to save this woman, a total stranger."

Maui, a Newfoundland, chose to risk his life to save three strangers, clinging to a surfboard off the coast of Corsica. The tourists had stupidly ignored red flags warning that the sea was too dangerous for swimming. Maui, blinking against salt water, paddled out to get them. As rough waves tossed him around like a matchstick, he managed to drag two of the tourists to shore. When he went back for the third, a huge wave slammed him underwater, and he disappeared. Later on the beach, no one could resuscitate him.

The denouement of this sorry episode is chilling: Once the

third tourist got safely to shore with the other two, whom Maui had saved, they all ran away. They showed no concern for the dog's fate. No gratitude that he had died for them. No kindness for the dog who had chosen to show total strangers such compassion.

Surely dogs like Trouble and Maui respond to the fear in others' voices, just as firemen hear people cry for help, then rush into burning buildings and rescue them. The same concern and eagerness to help drive the dogs' choice to show kindness. "Compassion rules dogs' existence," Jeff Masson, author of *Dogs Never Lie about Love*, once told me. "Dogs refuse to abide by the bystander effect." When others are in desperate straits, dogs don't stand around and think the situation has nothing to do with them. Nor do they consider that involvement could be too dangerous, as did Dawn hearing screams and a gunshot in Louisville, Ohio, or people watching Kitty Genovese's murder from their apartment windows in New York.

Genes and tit-for-tat paybacks don't even whisper on the sidelines of Maui and Trouble's dramatic and compassionate rescues of strangers. And the same can often be said about other species.

At Vancouver's Public Aquarium, for example, people saw a female killer whale share her food with seagulls. The kindness was reported in *Zoo Biology* and interpreted as "observational learning" or "social mimicry," meaning that the whale was not choosing to be compassionate but was simply copying the aquarium keepers' feeding of her.

The arrogance of this interpretation bothers me. The stories I've just related show how animals' kindness stems from their own empathy, not from behavior they've learned from humans. Rather than following our example, animals can act on their own feelings and impulses. I say this with confidence because, just as the whale fed the seagulls, animals in the *wild*, who have never been around people before, sometimes choose to show compassion to needy animals that they happen upon.

In *The Human Nature of Birds*, Theodore Xenophon Barber describes terns who lifted a flockmate, shot by hunters, out of danger; two at a time, they took his wings, moved him a few yards, and set him down again, repeating the process over and over. Barber also tells of a robin who crippled a male rival in a fight but afterward fed him and helped him stay alive. And a male blue jay led a human to a baby bird of a different species that had fallen from its nest; the jay then shared his food and "mothered" the baby until it grew up.

I was never so convinced about compassion in wildlife until I took a recent trip to Africa. Everywhere I went, in cities and in camps, I asked animal rehabilitation experts, guides, and conservationists if they'd ever seen wildlife being kind in the bush. I was amazed that everyone I talked with had at least one example. That made me wonder how much more animal compassion remains unwitnessed by humans.

Kerry Blewett, a manager at Vumbura Camp on Botswana's Okananga Delta, was driving along one night when her headlights shone on a male lion, feasting alone on a zebra kill. Standing a few feet away was a hippo, who seemed at first just to be biding his time at the side of the road. Farther away were six female lions, drooling as they waited for dinner.

Whenever they got too eager and crept toward the zebra, the hippo charged and ran them off—again and again, as Blewett watched, for an hour. Only when the male lion stood up and hobbled away did the compassion behind the scene become apparent. The lion's leg was severely injured, possibly broken. So crippled and in pain, he could not hunt or defend himself. The hippo had kept the females from devouring the zebra until the disabled male had gotten his fill.

Ronnie Watt, producer of a TV series called "Veldfocus" in Johannesburg, South Africa, gave me a video that showed another Good Samaritan hippo. While at the Mana Pools National Reserve in Zimbabwe, an impala was filmed sloshing around in the water without realizing that two crocodiles were silently swimming closer. One of the crocodiles snapped its teeth into the impala but not securely enough to haul it deeper for a kill. As the impala thrashed to free itself, a hippo, wallowing nearby with its pod, saw the fight and ran through the shallow water.

The crocodile was apparently frightened of a creature who could open its mouth a gaping 105 degrees and chomp with a ferocity as deadly as its own. The crocodile respectfully released its grip, and the hippo escorted the impala onto the bank, like a personal bodyguard.

Poniso Shamukuni, a guide at Chobe National Park in Botswana, witnessed another kindness to an impala, this one a newborn baby that was left alone and vulnerable when a cheetah scattered its herd. The cheetah slashed the baby's side and got ready to kill it, when two male baboons came running. They barked, bared their sharp teeth, and tried to bite the cheetah, who, like the rest of its species, was easily intimidated. It fled, and the baboons, mission accomplished, gently walked the baby impala back to its herd.

"I saw this with my own eyes," Shamukuni, shaking his head with wonder, told me. "There are so many mysteries in nature. We're only beginning to understand a small part of them."

There are also many examples of wild animals choosing to show compassion to humans. In *Mind of the Raven*, Bernd Heinrich describes a bird who cawed and cawed at a woman named Ginny Hannum. Working behind her cabin in Colorado's

Boulder Canyon, Hannum was unaware that a cougar had silently made its way to rocks twenty feet from her. It was crouched down in the shadows, its eyes riveted on her.

The raven kept cackling and cawing. An annoying pest, or so Hannum thought, it moved from three hundred yards away right up to her. It swooped down, then flew to the rocks, where the motion of wings must have made the cougar move its head slightly. Hannum saw it—just in time to run for help. She believes that the raven saved her life.

Some biologists hypothesize that birds lead animals to prey because once the animals have their fill, the birds can get the leftovers. That interpretation, which may be right in some cases, seems to give short shrift to the raven who warned Hannum. Maybe the raven was trying in its own bird way to show compassion, just like the terns who rescued their disabled flockmate. If helping the cougar find Hannum had been the raven's intent, it surely wouldn't have so boldly warned her that the cougar was approaching, then showed her its exact location.

Far better known than birds for volunteering compassion to people are dolphins, who have a long history of assisting drowning seafarers. Prehistoric Scandinavian art depicts dolphins not just saving lives but also helping fishermen find fish and navigate their boats. Aristotle wrote about dolphin rescues, as did an unfortunate classical Greek poet, Arion, whom sailors tossed overboard. Lucky for him, dolphins came along, swept him up, and carried him to shore.

More recent accounts show that dolphins are choosing to keep up this tradition of compassion. In a *Boston Globe* article, Steve Black reports that a group of dolphins tried to push the bow of his trimaran away from three humpback whales he was headed straight for on a solo trans-Atlantic trip. A British tourist in a *New York Times* article describes dolphins who fought off attacking sharks. As the tourist's blood spread out in the water and he screamed for help, the dolphins smacked their flippers and tails against the water's surface to keep the sharks from coming back. In the case of Elián Gonzáles, the five-year-old whose mother drowned during their escape from Cuba, fishermen apparently found the boy, clinging to an inner tube, surrounded by dolphins. Elián claimed that they'd broken waves for him and protected him from sharks for his two horrible days all alone in the ocean.

I've also read of a turtle who chose to offer this kindness at sea. After a shipwreck off the Manila coast, the turtle held a woman up on the water's surface for two days. And on a cold, foggy night, six gray seals swam up to Charlene Camburn as currents were carrying her off England's Lincolnshire Coast toward the open North Sea. Her hands were too cold to grab a seal and hang on, so the animals dove under her and prodded her legs and feet to make her bob up whenever she started to sink.

To me, even more astonishing than these compassionate rescues of people at sea are those rescues of what scientists call "feral children." I always thought that the story of the she-wolf who adopted Romulus and Remus was a myth. But after researching feral children, I'm not so sure. There are so many examples of wolves and other wild animals choosing to be kind to children that we can't dismiss the stories lightly.

Experts have confirmed some of the stories, including one of Ivan Mishukov, an abandoned six-year-old who was picked up by police in Reutova, west of Moscow. For two years, stray feral dogs had befriended the boy and, in Russia's bitter winter nights, had found warm spots for him to sleep with them in trash bins, the cellars and attics of vacant buildings, and near the hot water pipes in underground sewers.

Police tried for a month to get Ivan away from the dogs. Only when the police lured the dogs to some meat and shut a door behind them could they separate the little boy. The police took Ivan, screaming and biting, from his compassionate canine family.

Compassionate monkeys in Uganda adopted John Ssebunya, who as a toddler fled from his father, who had killed his mother. Traumatized, hungry, and frightened that he'd be his father's next victim, John wandered around the jungle for several days. A group of vervet monkeys brought him roots, nuts, fruits, sweet potatoes, and kasava, then slowly taught John to forage on his own, climb trees, and travel along branches with them.

Because Ugandans were fighting a civil war at that time, they stayed out of the depths of the jungle where John was living with the monkeys. But one day a villager named Millie went farther than she'd intended while gathering wood. In a forest clearing she noticed the monkeys and was startled to see that one of them had no tail. It was a boy, she realized, his nails so long that they curled around toward his palm, and his knees white and callused because he had been walking on them.

When the other villagers came to rescue John, their human faces scared him so badly that he threw sticks and climbed a tree to hide. The monkeys also fought to keep anyone from hurting the boy or taking him away. But they lost, and John went to the Kamuzinda Christian Orphanage near Kampala, where two teachers, Paul and Molly Wasswa, taught him to be human, to speak Swahili, and to take his strange circumstances with good humor.

Not having spoken words as a child, John stutters badly. This stuttering, along with his way of greeting monkeys he was put with to test his story, has led some experts to believe that he is an authentic feral child. John would not look at the test monkeys directly but glanced at them sideways, just as monkeys in the wild do with each other. Even today, ten years after Millie found John, he smiles by pulling his lips back and exposing his gums, as monkeys do. He holds things oddly between both wrists; and he lopes along unevenly when he walks—movements he learned from the monkeys who chose to be so compassionate to him.

John says he's grateful to the monkeys, whose kindness—in sharp contrast to the behavior of his father—saved his life. Recognizing his fear and loneliness in the jungle, the monkeys must have chosen to help. What could they have possibly had to gain from showing compassion to a human orphan?

Nothing. In this case, it's certainly hard to claim that animal altruism is always based on helping kin or getting paybacks.

For a magazine article several years ago, I interviewed David Sloan Wilson, a biology professor at New York's Binghamton University and co-author of *Unto Others: The Evolution and Psychology of Unselfish Behavior*. He understood why I was concerned that so many experts keep insisting that only humans are capable of real kindness, and animals are not. "There's no reason to think that compassion would be uniquely human because it doesn't have much to do with brainpower," Wilson reassured me. "It's more reflexive and emotional. The deeply emotional things are shared by many species."

Because we do share at our core so many basic feelings with animals, I would think we can also learn from them about compassion. What we might learn is how simple and pure compassion can be. Animals can dispense it so freely. For them, being kind hasn't become a convoluted act—carried out with niggardliness and hesitation—as it has for many of us.

Animal compassion is spontaneous. When animals feel empathy, they dive right in and are kind without a backward glance. Their compassion is whole-hearted, all-or-nothing, damn-the-torpedoes. It has an extraordinary economy. Animals don't fritter away kindness by offering it when it's not wanted or needed. Their compassion is so basic and direct; nothing is wasted or forced on others.

Knuks, a ferret, is beautifully compassionate in this way. Her name is "skunk" spelled backward because, as a baby, she had a black stripe down her white back and was a skunk in reverse. She lives with Mary Shefferman, editor-in-chief of *Modern Ferret Magazine*, and nine other ferrets, one of whom, Sabrina, went blind in her old age and had a rough time when Shefferman moved them all to a new home.

On fearful trips outside her cage, Sabrina would inch her way around the wall, her whiskers touching baseboards, as if she were trying to get an understanding of the room. Whenever she tried to walk across it, the old ferret would run straight into table legs and chairs.

Her constant struggle did not go unnoticed by Knuks. At first, each time Sabrina thumped into something, Knuks hurried to escort her around it. Then Knuks began to accompany Sabrina all over the room to help her learn the new location of each piece of furniture. She also began to anticipate when Sabrina would hit something; and so when Sabrina was heading for a table leg, Knuks would gently steer her to less dangerous territory.

When you remember that animals like Knuks have no hands or speech—and that animals are extremely limited in the ways they can show kindness—it's amazing how the kindness they *do* choose to extend to others is so appropriate and exactly tailored to their needs. Looking after an old, blind friend in this simple and earnest way, it seems to me, is the height of compassion. Though restricted in so many ways, animals give so freely. If only we could all do the same.

3.

COURAGE

Two days after Beauty, a chestnut mare, gave birth to her foal, Sultan, the winter weather turned bitter cold. And the Jan du Toit's River, which flowed through the South African farm where Beauty lived, turned into a torrent of rushing, foaming water.

In freezing rain, Hank Gorter went to find Beauty and Sultan in the afternoon to bring them to their stable. But, apparently, horses whinnying on the other side of the river were more compelling than a warm barn; Beauty and Sultan leapt into the dangerous water and swam across to join them. In the strong current, Beauty nudged Sultan along and kept him steady. Just as the foal climbed out, however, the muddy riverbank collapsed and he fell back, neighing with terror, into the water.

With all her strength, Beauty paddled through the raging current and tried to reach Sultan before he was carried downstream to his death. Gorter ran down the bank and also tried to grab the foal as the water took him away, but Gorter slipped and was swept into the torrent, too. Sputtering for air, he bobbed to the surface next to Beauty, whose eyes, he remembers, were bulging in fear. In spite of her panic, Beauty stopped trying to get to Sultan just long enough to shove Gorter with her nose toward the safety of the riverbank. As Gorter clung to tree roots, Beauty finally reached her foal and guided him to an island in the middle of the river.

When Beauty behaved so valiantly in such terrifying circumstances, it's impossible for us to know with certainty what was on her mind. Perhaps she was acting impulsively, like a human mother who doesn't think of herself for an instant when her child is in trouble; she does whatever she has to do, including dying herself, to save her child. On the other hand, Beauty also stopped her efforts on behalf of her foal to rescue Gorter, whom she barely knew, in spite of Sultan's desperate situation and her own danger. That seems to me to be a deliberate—and even moral—choice. When Beauty acted as she did, she clearly showed great courage.

If people risk their lives to help someone, we don't seem to care if they're acting on impulse or choice. The outcome is the same: These heroes are congratulated for their bravery and showered with accolades. But bravery is bravery, whether shown by a person or a horse, and I believe that animals should be recognized in this way, too. So often, though, animals' courage goes unacknowledged. Or it's dismissed, negated, or explained away as something else.

That isn't fair. In circumstances that might leave many of us immobilized with fear, animals can choose to act in amazing ways, especially when they help their human guardians. But researchers often dismiss animal courage, by saying, simply, that animals don't feel fear. Since winning a victory over fear is usually the basis of courage, then animals can't be called brave, or so the argument goes.

"Fear is an inference. We don't know anything about animals' direct experience, if anything," explains Peter Lang, a research professor of clinical and health psychology at the University of Florida. When I asked him if animals' pounding hearts and trembling bodies weren't physical signals of fear (as they are with us), he said that "physiological signs don't tell us what animals are experiencing." In other words, when an animal displays those signs, it may be showing only an automatic biological response, not an emotional one. Fear is out of the picture.

But from laboratory experiments, other experts have concluded that animals *can* be fearful.

For one thing, certain drugs seem to bring fear out in some species. In several studies, researchers rewarded rats for pressing a bar in threatening situations but did not reward them for pressing it in nonthreatening ones. After the researchers then gave the rats a drug called pentaline tetrazol (PTZ), the rats pressed the bar just as they did when threatened. When the rats have taken PTZ, "they feel scared. In other words, there is a consistent, subjective experience associated with fear," explains Caroline Blanchard, a research professor at the University of Hawaii's Pacific Biomedical Research Center. "On the basis of these subjective effects, the rats can determine that the situation [with the drug] is more similar to when they're scared than to when they're not scared."

Certain situations also seem to draw fear out of experimental animals. If lab rats are allowed to live happily for generations with nothing to fear, and then researchers set even a gentle, well-behaved cat near them for fifteen minutes, says Blanchard, "you change those rats' lives for a long, long time. Before, they never realized that anything was scary. But now they know. For at least the next several days, those guys are really nervous." The rats stick their heads out of their burrowing tunnels and cautiously sniff and look around for the cat before venturing out. They eat less, drink less, and have less sex. "Now they're worried," Blanchard adds. "The fear is built in them, only requiring certain types of stimuli to release it."

If chickens are faced with something unfamiliar, they can show fear, too. In a study at the Victorian Institute of Animal Science in Australia, researcher John Barnett studied the position and posture of hens when someone stood close to their cages. The person's sex, height, or eyeglasses seemed not to phase the hens at all. But they crouched down or tried to escape when the person wore overalls instead of their usual clothes. Barnett concluded that the birds were not accustomed to seeing overalls; that novelty, which they sensed as danger, apparently, set off a fearful reaction.

Outside of labs, other experts have observed animals' behavior and determined that they can be afraid of many things. Bob Andrysco, a pet behaviorist in Columbus, Ohio, has worked with dogs who cowered at firecrackers, thunder, people wearing hats, and a window that a burglar had once come through. One dog whined and ran to hide from lights reflected on walls. Another dog would tremble at the sight of blimps. A cat, threatened by unfamiliar people in his home, sank his claws into a visitor's anklebone and refused to let loose for twenty agonizing minutes. By recognizing danger in this way, Andrysco says, the cat was "like a person getting so afraid during a scary TV movie that he grabs and holds a pillow."

What better way is there for animals to tell us of their fear than by their behavior? And what could make the fear more obvious than their trembling, crouching, or trying to run? The signs of animal fear are too apparent to ignore, as are stories of animals who have overcome fear and, in so doing, demonstrated its opposite: courage. Yet several experts, including those who give animals credit for being afraid, winced when I suggested that animals could be brave. That concept seemed out of the question.

Once again we have to decide for ourselves if we should go along with widely accepted expert opinion—or, specifically, if we might conclude that animals can override their fears and be courageous. In many of the stories I've collected, I see no other way of interpreting the action of the animals except to see it in these terms.

One such animal was Ole, a chocolate Lab, known for being so timid and fearful that he'd take cover, like a prairie dog, every time that hawks flew overhead. When chased by a moose once, he ran and hid his head between the legs of his guardian, Stan Anderson. With ears like flaps on a hunter's cap and fur glossy as a seal, Ole seemed to have the courage of

Ole

toast—until one hike he and Anderson took near Rex Ford, Montana.

As man and dog walked along a grassy logging road, a black bear cub trundled out of the woods. Anderson's stomach squeezed into a knot of apprehension. Sure that the cub's mother would undoubtedly show up in a minute, Anderson whispered to Ole, "Let's get out of here." But before they could turn and run, the mother bear rose out of a ditch a hundred feet away.

Rearing up on her hind legs to a menacing six feet, the bear charged and swept her paw across Anderson's face. Blood poured down his cheek, and he was sure he'd lost an eye. He was also sure he'd soon be dead; Ole, always so fearful, couldn't possibly be brave enough to come to his aid. But Ole snarled and barked and snapped at the bear. He clamped his teeth into her leg with such ferocity, in fact, that she paused for an instant, perhaps wondering if killing Anderson with this fierce dog around was more trouble than it was worth. She turned and loped back to her cub.

About to go into shock, Anderson staggered, bleeding, toward his car. It was parked a mile away, and he wasn't sure he could make it that far and then drive the five miles home. Things got even worse when he heard scratching in the earth behind him, then felt breath on the back of his neck. Dread flashing through his mind, he braced himself.

The mother bear rammed her head against Anderson and bit his shoulder, then grabbed his elbow in her teeth and, with a terrible grinding sound, champed clear to his bone. Ole went crazy. Barking, yowling, and snapping, he hurled himself at the bear and bit any part of her that he could reach.

Anderson, as terrified for Ole as for himself, shoved the bear with his free arm in a last desperate attempt to turn her away. Thrown off balance, she momentarily unclamped her jaw, and

Ole sank his teeth into her hindquarters. She whirled around and again lumbered back to her cub as Ole kept barking. All his life Ole had been a fierce closet gladiator, Anderson realized, and not a trembling butterfly.

When they finally reached the car, Ole set aside his new bravery and ferocity and again became his usual gentle, sensitive self. He plastered his body against Anderson and supported him, then licked his face to keep him from passing out on the drive home. Anderson, who required hundreds of stitches for his wounds, says, "Ole was determined to save me. He knew what he was doing." Thrown into a crisis, he went against his basic, fearful nature and mustered the courage to do what he knew needed to be done.

Researchers' arguments to the contrary, plenty of animals, like Ole, find themselves in dangerous situations, feel fear, and choose to override it. And when they do, it seems to me that we owe them an honest appraisal of their action. They deserve to be called "brave."

Experts dismiss animal courage in another way: What might look like bravery, they argue, is just a reflex, based on involuntary physiological responses to a stimulus. Danger is said to trigger the reflex, or "defensive behavior," which is an animal's way of protecting itself, or occasionally its family or pack, from threats. Courage has nothing to do with the defense, presumably. The behavior is said to be a predictable, automatic biological process.

In the first step of the defense process, an animal recognizes danger, usually by smell or sight. Sometimes the recognition is learned through bad experiences. A deer who's been slightly injured by a car while crossing a road may learn to bolt from the road when it sees another car coming. At other times, the recognition is instinctive; lab rats, for instance, become instantly wary of a fox's smell even if they've never seen a fox before.

Once danger is perceived, the animal reflexively freezes, immobile, while attentively watching and gathering information. At the same time, involuntary physiological changes in the animal's brain and body prepare it, if need be, for taking defensive action.

The first sniff of danger sends messages along nerve pathways from the animal's nose to its amygdala, an almond-shaped structure just below the brain's cortex. Then the danger signals move on to other parts of the brain—the stria terminalis, the hypothalamus, the periaqueductal gray matter of the midbrain. Where the signal travels makes a difference: Different systems control different types of defensive behavior—whether, for instance, the animal will run away, bite, claw, kick, or shriek in defense.

An awareness of danger also automatically causes an animal's brain to release chemicals and hormones that enhance the defensive action that the animal will take. When the hypothalamus receives danger signals, the pituitary gland sends ACTH, or andrenocorticotropic hormone, through the blood to the adrenal glands. That triggers adrenaline to travel to receptors in different parts of the body. With the release of adrenaline, an animal's heart beats faster, so blood pressure increases, and more blood gets pumped through the body. That carries extra oxygen and glucose to the places the animal needs for a swift and strong defense.

An increase in blood to the animal's arm and leg muscles allows for stronger, quicker physical motion. More blood flowing to the paws and feet causes the excretion of sweat for better traction. And increased blood flow to the eyes makes the pupils dilate for sharper vision. With the help of adrenaline, an animal's body is physiologically ready for the last part of the process: fight or flight.

Whether the animal confronts a threat or runs away, the prevailing scientific view is that the animal is still only operating on automatic reflex and being driven by adrenaline; there is no thought—and certainly no courage or choice—behind the animal's action. I believe, however, that this is exactly the point at which courage or choice can enter the picture. I say this by looking at what the animals *do*.

In a perfect example of freely chosen and courageous flight, two orphaned sister brown bear cubs ran for their lives on Siberia's Kamchatka Peninsula. Naturalist Charlie Russell watched with binoculars as a vicious predator male, who had earlier killed and eaten another cub, came after them. For miles, the cubs fled over a frozen lake, then back toward shore, up over a mountaintop, down into a gully, and back toward the lake again. Just as the male bear reached out to grab one of the cubs, her sister, who could have escaped, chose to turn with great daring and shoot across the predator's path. Her move, surely no reflex, took enormous courage and distracted him just long enough for her sister to run and save herself.

Zoologist Jon Rood once saw an example of freely chosen and courageous fight when an eagle snatched one of a pack of mongoose and flew with it to a tree in Tanzania's Serengeti National Park. The pack's dominant male, surely desperate to save his pack member, charged up the trunk with several other mongoose close behind, a small army on a rescue mission facing impossible odds. As the captured mongoose struggled for its life in the eagle's talons, the lead mongoose lunged boldly and repeatedly at the huge raptor, who could have shredded him in seconds. At the brave attack, the eagle dropped its prey, unhurt, to the ground.

For we humans, it doesn't take much to imagine the emotions of the cub who cut in front of the attacking male bear, or the mongoose who fought the eagle. Like the cub, we may have seen a menacing opponent and run in terror for our lives—and possibly tried to help someone escape with us. Like the mongoose, we might have watched someone we love face an assailant right in front of us, and we've furiously gathered our wits and strength to fight and help.

As humans, we can also easily understand the physiological responses going on inside the bear cub and the mongoose because, in dangerous situations, we have similar responses. Explains psychologist Peter Lang, "All the structures [for defense] are in the older part of the brain. We share them with most mammals, and we have the same reflexes." So on our most primitive mental level we know, as well as the bear cub and the mongoose did, about rapid heartbeats, sweaty hands, and blood pounding at our temples.

If in dangerous situations, our emotions and physiology may be similar to animals, why is it said that only we are capable of bravery and animals are not? And why are animals in danger usually seen as driven only by adrenaline and not by thought or choice?

No matter how frantically an animal tries to help or what terrifying situations it takes on, I've been told, it's just acting as we do when we jump in automatically to rescue someone and, only later, after the person is safe, feel our knees go wobbly at the realization of what we've done. On these occasions, we've acted without considering consequences or evaluating risks. "In high adrenaline situations, we often don't think. There's no reason to assume that animals have any different responses," says Emily Weiss, curator of behavior and research at Sedgwick County Zoo in Wichita, Kansas.

We call ourselves brave when we risk our lives for others without thinking about what we're doing, so surely animals can be said to be brave when they do the same. Consciously choosing or not choosing an action does not negate the courage behind it. Furthermore, we know that we do *not* always act on impulse when we face danger; sometimes we consider a threat and then decide, anyway, to move ahead into the thick of it to help someone—and we definitely call that courage. Animals must also sometimes make the same choice to take risks for others. And, when they do, they certainly are brave.

Animals' choice is apparent, for example, when they willingly face danger for an extended period and not for what might be taken as a reflexive flash of action. Animals who risk their safety for a longer rescue have time to consider what they're doing, and yet they still choose to continue. And that takes courage.

Driving on a highway in Hawaii, Anne Frisch, national coordinator for the Coalition to Protect Canadian Geese, happened to come upon a pair of geese, a male and a female. The birds' wings had been clipped, so they'd had to waddle, rather than fly, across the highway to get to better grass. The female was hit by a car and badly injured. To keep her safe from cars that whizzed past dangerously close, the male spread his wings around her so protectively that Frisch could scarcely see her. With nothing but a beak for a weapon, he stood there for many long and frightening minutes and bravely tried to defend her.

The male goose knew what he was doing. As the cars sped past, he felt the wind that they created ruffle his feathers, and he heard the fearsome grinding of motors and roaring of tires. He also was well aware of the body of another goose lying nearby; a car had killed it as it had tried to cross the highway, too. But in spite of the danger, the male bravely kept his arms around his injured female companion and chose to risk his life to stay with her for as long as necessary. Even when Frisch stopped her car, and she and other pedestrians slowly approached, the male goose did not shrink back and desert his friend at the potential threat of oncoming humans. He stayed and stayed, unyielding.

The argument that animals are only responding reflexively to a physiological urge and adrenaline rush when they seem to be brave cannot apply in every situation. All we have to do is think about that goose, who chose to confront danger for an extended time and showed the best of courage. So many other animals have done the same.

One type of courage demonstrated by animals is the courage of protection. And, more than in any other situation, animals bravely try to protect others in fire. Smoke, flames, and heat are uncomfortable, unfamiliar, and anxiety producing—even terrifying—to animals. They're well aware of the danger fire presents, and yet I've collected, in just the last two years, sixty-six newspaper stories of all kinds of animals often risking their lives and bravely trying to alert people to the threat of it.

On one occasion, Honeymoon, a New Jersey pig, oinked and shrieked and kicked at a door to wake his human family to flames. Charlie, a parrot in England, imitated a child in the family by squawking "help!" to let his guardians know they were in danger. Snowball, a hamster, made such a disturbance by rustling around loudly in his cage that his Connecticut family bolted up in bed and found fire shooting from a wall. When a house in Australia caught fire, a kangaroo, just rescued from the pouch of his dead mother, pounded boldly on a bedroom door to wake the man who'd saved him.

When cats bravely try to wake someone to fire, they use a

range of techniques. They meow, shriek, and howl, or they frantically knead chests, rub against people's faces, and tickle them
with whiskers. If that doesn't work, cats fearlessly jump up and
down on people, as did one Kansas City feline who raced, wail-
ing, from bedroom to bedroom and took a running leap, square
on the chest, of all five people in the house. Cats have been
known to hook their claws into the flesh of sleeping people to
roust them out of bed in fires. In Pittsburgh, Pennsylvania, a
usually gentle Abyssinian named Dolores, scratched Kyle
Leibach's face until he woke. When he got to the back door of his
house, the knob came off in his hand. He collapsed to the floor
from smoke inhalation, and, to revive him, Dolores scratched
him all over again.

Courageous dogs scratch at bedroom doors, whimper, bark,
yowl, pace, and run from bedroom to bedroom to alert members
of a family to fire. They lick, nudge, then bite—or more. Kane, a
125-pound Great Dane in Palm Beach Gardens, Florida, jumped,
howling, on top of her sleeping guardian to alert her to flames.
Bandit, an Australian shepherd in Daytona Beach, Florida,
grabbed David Carey's ankle in his teeth and dragged his
guardian off the bed where he'd been sleeping. Then Bandit led
Carey and his wife to the front door. Instead of running out to
save himself, the dog stopped and turned his head back toward
the house. Realizing that Bandit wanted him to rescue their cat,
Carey followed the brave dog inside again and saved it.

Animal behaviorists have told me that animals who alert people to fires in the night are not necessarily showing courage or
concern for others. In an interview several years ago, Bonnie
Beaver, a professor in the Department of Small Animal Medicine
and Surgery at Texas A&M University, said that cats in fires
"will often go to the person who knows how to open the door and

get them out—and the cats coincidentally happen to save the person." In other words, when animals try so hard to wake someone, all they want is to get themselves to safety.

This may be true in some cases. But in others, the animals are undoubtedly choosing to be brave and do all they can to help. Dogs who are outside in the yard, for instance, are often known to bark themselves hoarse to wake people inside burning houses—instead of running away from the flames themselves. And dogs inside a burning house have risked their lives to pull people toward doors, so the people—clearly not just the dog— can escape. Duke, a black Lab in Bangs, Texas, woke his family to a fire, then bravely refused to go outside to save himself until all the children had first gotten out safely.

Aldo, a Great Dane, herded his human family out of a burning condominium in Port Hueneme, California. As the three adults stood outside watching the blaze, they realized the dog had disappeared. He'd gone back inside to get two other people. Firemen later found Aldo, unconscious, in a smoke-filled bedroom, with flames flickering around him. He eventually revived.

Demonstrations of courage from a huge two-hundred-pound adult dog like Aldo may not be surprising. But Misty, a small, six-month-old field spaniel puppy, showed that she was just as brave. Misty was asleep in her guardian's Quaker Hill, Connecticut house when a television set exploded in the living room and shattering glass woke the entire family. Brian and Kim Rouisse rushed outside with their newborn baby. Kim's mother, sister, and brother climbed out of their second-floor bedrooms onto the roof. Kim's father, Bob Schlink, a firefighter by profession, hurried out of the basement and grabbed a garden hose to put out flames. Misty shot out of the house and stood by the back door. Only the Rouisse's two-year-old son, Alex, who was mildly autistic, was unaccounted for.

"It was pitch black, 1:30 in the morning," Kim remembers. "You couldn't see. You couldn't breathe from all the smoke. Neighbors had their air conditioners running, so no one heard us screaming." No one came to help.

As Kim ran to a neighbor to call 9-1-1, Brian and Bob searched frantically for Alex. Misty kept trying to shove back into the house through the door into the kitchen, but Brian and Bob kept pushing her away. Finally, desperate, she broke through and tore straight into the burning living room. Bob ran after her.

He found Misty only because her neon-pink collar glowed in the smoke. With flames all around her, she was sitting under the dining room table beside Alex. Unable to talk or save himself, the toddler was hiding in terror; but Misty bravely guarded and comforted him while they waited for someone to help.

"If an animal runs into flames, it has a good reason to do so because, without question, flames are something it's scared of," says biomedical researcher Caroline Blanchard. When I asked Kim Rouisse what Misty's reason might have been, she said, "She loves Alex, and he loves her. She acted exactly like a mother would, going in to get one of her kids." The motive behind Misty's courage was concern.

Zoo curator Emily Weiss sees it differently. Dogs are extremely loyal pack animals, who can read moods and recognize distress, which distresses them, as well, she says. In the fire Misty may have heard Alex cry or smelled his fear and gotten stressed. As a result, "she would be more comfortable near her pack than off by herself," Weiss theorizes. "Being with the pack has more of a calming effect than being away from it."

That may be true. But in all the heat and flames and screams that night, Misty surely would have found the greatest calm as far as possible from the fire, or at least with an adult in her "pack" who could protect her, not with a child she herself had to protect. Returning to Alex surely required overcoming enormous discomfort and fear—and displaying undeniable courage.

As with fire rescues, I've also collected many stories of water rescues when animals, especially dogs, freely demonstrate the courage of protection. In order to help someone about to drown, animals will often control their natural aversion to, or fear of, water. Dogs have dived into swollen creeks or rushing rivers and offered their fur or collars to people as lifelines. Or dogs have taken people's limbs or clothing in their teeth and towed them to shore. Leiah, a malamute puppy in Victoria, British Columbia, once ran down a ramp leading to a beach and bravely swam out into the water toward what looked like a clump of debris. It turned out to be a woman, a stranger to the dog. As the woman floated, nearly dead, in the waves, the little pup stayed with her and licked her face to revive her until help came.

Part of the courage in rescues like these is that the dogs involved could so easily have drowned, and they surely must have known it. Yet they jumped in anyway. In South Africa, Tasha, a very pregnant Stratfordshire bull terrier, got into the family's swimming pool and buoyed up a two-year-old boy—until, exhausted, she herself almost went under. In Marion, Louisiana, Sadie, a small, adolescent chocolate Lab, helped two people, who were fighting for their lives in a pond. Sadie did this while tied to a sinking rowboat that could easily have pulled her down to death.

This crisis started when the boat Sadie was in flipped over and threw her, twelve-year-old Frankie Pitts, and a mutt named Murphy into the water, just as Frankie's mother, Tammy, happened to look out her kitchen window. Tammy rushed outside, jumped into the pond in her running suit and sneakers, and swam toward the boat, her mind racing with horrifying possibilities. The pond was fourteen feet deep, way over Frankie's head. In February, the water was also freezing cold, an easy invitation to hypothermia. Frankie was wearing a winter coat; once water-logged, it would weigh him down and drown him. Worst of all, Murphy was so frightened that he was trying to climb on top of Frankie to save himself. The dog's weight was pushing Frankie's head below the water's surface.

Sadie's leash had been tied to an oarlock for safety, and now, towing the sinking boat, she paddled anxiously around Frankie and Murphy. When Tammy finally reached Frankie, the boy grabbed her left shoulder in a panic, and they both went under. As Tammy popped back up, Sadie was looking at her. "Her eyes were wide with fear," Tammy remembers. "She knew something was terribly wrong."

Sadie swam around Frankie so that Tammy could grab the dog without letting go of her son. As Murphy swam off to save himself, Sadie, who could easily have done the same, allowed Tammy to hold her collar with one hand and Frankie's sodden jacket with the other. Slowly, with all her strength, Sadie, who weighs just fifty pounds, courageously swam to the bank, drag-ging Tammy, Frankie, *and* the heavy, half-submerged boat behind her. "Sadie kept her cool and faced the danger of drowning, her-self," Tammy Pitts says. "I believe she'd do the same if the situa-tion ever came again. I know she'd give her life for us."

What's so interesting about this story is that Murphy paddled away after Frankie couldn't save him; but Sadie bravely stayed to help the boy. I asked zoo curator Emily Weiss, who once tested dogs for fearfulness while selecting shelter dogs as service animals, how two dogs could vary so greatly in courage. In tests she conducted, Weiss had opened an umbrella in front of the shelter dogs, or held out an odd wooden statue of a creature that looked like a wide-eyed hedgehog, or banged a spoon against a pan. She was trying to see if the dogs would cower, run to hide, or accept the movement, creature, or noise with aplomb.

What Weiss learned, she says, is that when it comes to fearfulness, "dogs vary, absolutely." Some are born with it genetically hardwired into their brains. Others develop it—or they develop fear*less*ness—according to what happens to them during the "sensitive period" of their lives that ranges from four to twenty-four weeks of age. In that time, says Weiss, "what experiences an animal has will have a great effect on its traits—whether it will be bold and confident or submissive and fearful."

Genes and environment during the sensitive period influence brain development and personality in animals, just as in human children, though the sensitive period of humans is thought to last for a longer time. Though both nature and nurture contributed to the development of Murphy's timidity and Sadie's courage, Sadie still *chose* to behave so bravely.

In addition to rescues from fire and water, the courage of protection is evident when animals bravely take on frightening opponents who are attacking someone or something that the animals are attached to. I have collected stories of geese defending children from huge, rabid dogs, and elephants and cows forming a circle around their keepers to stop rampaging bulls from hurting them. Eighteen cats in an apartment near Cairo, Egypt, recently attacked policemen after they broke in to investigate a smell. The officers had to defend themselves against hundreds of claws for two *hours* before they could retrieve the dead body of the cats' guardian, Bahgat Mostafa Said, whom they were bravely protecting.

Mostly, though, courageous protection comes from ordinary

dogs, no matter how small they are or how unequal the fight is going to be. Tara, a thirty-pound mongrel in southern California, snarled and lunged to hold off a mountain lion until her guardian could escape into his house trailer. Baxter, a miniature dachshund in Louisiana, took on a deer that was brandishing sharp antlers at his guardian. Bo, a brave cockapoo, tore out of his house on the outskirts of Philadelphia and jumped on two pit bulls who were attacking a boy, passing through Bo's neighborhood on his way home from school. In the process of helping a stranger, the dog suffered severe injuries.

Coach, a Border collie, was herding his human family along on a hike near Oshawa, Canada. As the group approached a fallen tree far ahead on the trail, no one but Coach saw a wasps' nest hidden among the branches. Barking, he ran and threw himself on it. The family believes he did so in order to get the wasps to go after him before Megan McQuoid, the family's eight-year-old child, walked closer to the nest. With angry wasps swarming around him, Coach rolled through the brush and jumped into a creek. There were at least fifty stings on his muzzle and belly. Megan didn't have one.

Even strays can show the courage of protection. One such dog, a blond mutt, wandered into a neighborhood in Sand Springs, Oklahoma, where residents yelled and threw stones to keep her away. She was covered with mange, her chest was bald, raw, unsightly, and she was starving. With bones sticking out beneath her pitiful tufts of fur, she chewed rocks in people's yard to stave off hunger.

Someone reported the dog to the sheriff, who decided her condition was too grim for her to be taken to a nearby shelter, where she might infect other animals with mange. So, from a distance, he shot her behind the ear, the usual way of disposing of sick, stray animals. The shot didn't kill the dog, however, and she staggered away, bleeding profusely. For the next three rainy days, residents in the neighborhood assumed she was dead.

But late one night, Renee Manor found a dog sitting by her mailbox. Noting the blood on the dog's head, Manor knew that the pathetic creature was the one who'd been shot. Sickened by the abuse, Manor fed the stray, removed her ticks, cleaned her wound with antiseptic spray, and allowed her to live on the front porch while Manor tried to find a home for her. There were no takers.

One afternoon, about a week later, Manor took her toddler daughter, Lexee, outside to play. As Lexee sniffed flowers and squatted down to pick one, the dog sidled up for petting and attention. Then Manor heard a rattle. Before the woman ever even saw the snake, however, the dog leapt up and knocked Lexee out of the way. The snake struck the dog's paw instead of Lexee's face. Yelping in pain, the dog ran under a nearby van, where she whimpered and licked the wound.

Several animal behaviorists have told me that dogs are drawn to snakes, not by an eagerness to defend someone, but by curiosity and what's called "visual stimulation." The movement of the snake supposedly attracts a dog who grabs it in his mouth on reflex. But the dog who protected Lexee can't be viewed as that kind of a machine only responding to a stimulus. No dumb, curious animal, this starving stray went after the child instead of the snake and shoved Lexee away to keep her safe. Manor named the dog Hero.

Another dog who bravely chose to protect someone from a formidable opponent was Pink. Pink's veterinarian, Jackie Cole, calls her "a classic golden retriever" and "the embodiment of sweetness and light," and all animal lovers know exactly the kind of timid, docile creature this describes: a lamb in dog's clothing, the type one might expect to roll over, submissive, at the sight of a housefly.

Every day Pink's guardian, Mark Muhich, would take her to the beach near his home in Galveston, Texas. She would sit beside him and watch while he did yoga on the sand. Early one evening as a big, orange sun was slowly sinking to the horizon, Muhich finished his stretches, lay on his back, and studied the sky. Suddenly Pink growled. She leapt over Muhich and, fur bristling, landed a few feet to his left. She planted her feet, snarled, barked, and jutted out her jaw. Her eyes shone, Muhich says, with the "brave resolve of someone facing down an enemy."

As Muhich jerked up his head to see what Pink saw, a Ford truck roared across the sand straight at him. Muhich hadn't heard it approaching from the left because he was deaf in his left ear. Clearly the driver didn't see him lying on the beach. As the truck zoomed closer, at forty miles an hour, the setting sun had shone into the driver's eyes and blinded him.

The vehicle was coming too fast for Muhich to show himself, much less get up and run. Pink, no gentle, fearful lamb now, stood between him and the truck, and barked and yowled as if she were ready to fight the entire world. Just a few feet away, the driver finally saw her. He slammed on his brakes and veered to keep from hitting the dog—so close that sand spewed all over her and Muhich. The driver missed Pink by only a couple of inches and Muhich by just a couple of feet.

As if nothing had happened, the driver kept going down the beach (where motor vehicles were prohibited, by the way). "He never even saw me," Muhich remembers. If Pink hadn't bravely chosen to put herself in the truck's path and gotten the driver's attention, he would have run over Muhich in an instant. To protect him, the normally sweet and timid dog took on a loud, fast-moving vehicle, vastly larger than she was.

In addition to protecting people from live or mechanical "predators," animals can also display courage when they protect people from other people, who may be far more dangerous than angry wasps, startled rattlesnakes, or even oncoming trucks. Newspapers frequently report stories of animals fighting off muggers, robbers, rapists, and kidnappers. When, for example, a burglar in southern China was heading for the door of a house with a family's safe, the owner, Sham Man-ling, came home and got into a kicking, screaming brawl with him. Mimi, Man-ling's Persian cat, sprang from a shelf and clawed the robber, who ran away.

Mack, a parrot, was just as courageous. When a criminal named John Rodriguez tried to steal tools from D'Light, a store

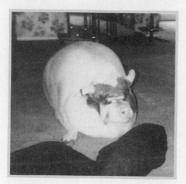

Tunia

in Glendale, California, Mack, who lived at the store, jumped on him, pecked, and squawked. In self-defense, Rodriguez yanked out Mack's feathers, hit the bird's head, and threw him, unconscious, to the ground. Still, Mack won the battle: He detained Rodriguez long enough for police to respond to the store's burglar alarm.

Then there's Tunia, short for Petunia, a great, white, four-hundred-pound pig who lives in the house of Kim and Glen Herron in Goose Creek, South Carolina. Tunia is supremely pampered; she's shampooed weekly, fed popsicles in the summer, and given plump pillows to sleep on. Because of all this kindness, Tunia is devoted to her family.

When Herron was folding laundry in the bedroom one afternoon, Tunia pricked up her ears and charged into the living room. With fierce urgency, she barked, as she'd learned to do from a neighbor dog. Then Tunia ran into the kitchen and banged her snout against the back door. When Herron pulled back the curtain covering the glass, she understood why the pig was so upset.

Herron's breath stuck in her throat. A man was standing on the porch, staring menacingly back at her. His reason for being at her door was clearly not benign. Frozen in terror, Herron was also scared for Tunia, who kept hurling herself against the glass. If it broke, the pig could cut herself; and if she knocked the whole door down, she might hurt herself far worse. To stop Tunia's frantic pounding, Herron opened the door and let the pig out.

Snapping and barking like the world's meanest dog, Tunia chased the intruder around trees and flowerbeds in the backyard and, finally, cornered him on a box beside the yard's chain-link fence. The man jumped over the fence and ran away. Says Herron, "Tunia's my brave girl."

Brandy with Kendall Plank

An even braver girl was a feisty little English springer spaniel pup named Brandy. Her breed—originally named because the dogs "sprang" from cover to flush out game—was meant to work as gun dogs. But even a temperament that's supposed to be unfazed by shots still cannot explain Brandy's extraordinary courage when her guardian, Kendall

Plank, home alone one night, woke to the bark of neighborhood dogs—and feet crunching on gravel just outside her window.

Someone turned the wrought iron door handle to get into Plank's entryway. Finding it locked, the intruder walked around to the bathroom window. Plank hurried out of bed and called 9-1-1 as Brandy watched, silent and extremely serious. "She was attending to me," Plank remembers. Just a few months old, the pup seemed to be looking to Plank for signals about how to respond to what was happening.

With a portable phone in her hand, Plank walked out of her bedroom down the hallway, where she'd left on a light. So frightened that she could barely make words come through her lips, she whispered to an emergency dispatcher that someone was breaking into her house. Then Plank called her sister, who tried to calm her until the police arrived. Plank heard a crash in the bathroom and knew the intruder had gotten inside. Now she was totally vulnerable.

Down the hall, two inches of a machine-gun barrel came slowly around the corner. Then four inches. Six. A man stepped in front of Plank. He put the gun on his hip and shot her in the arm. As she sank to the floor, he shot her in the back.

Brandy, who weighed less than thirty pounds, could easily have run away or cowered somewhere out of sight. Instead, barking and snarling, the little dog sprang on the man and tore through the house after him as he tried to run away. The man shot Brandy five times—in her jaw, hip, chest, leg, and upper body—but she kept chasing and yapping. Even as bullets came at her and ricocheted off walls, she bit his arm and finally chased him to the bathroom.

When the intruder jumped back out the bathroom window, police were waiting, and they shot and killed him. Brandy, covered with blood and nearly in shock, managed to get to Plank.

"She knew something was wrong, and I was in pain," Plank says, "and she wanted to help me."

After miraculously surviving her wounds, for the next three months Brandy insisted on sleeping under the bathroom window at night. Says Plank, "For a long time, she was still guarding me." Though she'd already shown more courage than the burliest Marine, the little dog continued to be brave.

In addition to the courage of protection, animals also exhibit a second kind of courage, what I call the courage of work. With this kind of bravery, animals willingly face dangerous day-to-day jobs in order to do what is asked of them and please their employer. Well aware of risks to their personal safety, animals will nevertheless plow ahead to help others whom they've never met and never will. Animals sometimes even appear eager to do a frightening job courageously.

Maggie is one brave cat who seems almost to have chosen her tough work. Found in a dumpster as a tiny, unweaned kitten, she was raised by a staff member at the Pasadena, California Humane Society and S.P.C.A., then returned to the shelter to live. Maggie seemed blasé about the dogs who came and went until once, when no one could decide if a particular stray was a gentleman or a brute with cats, someone suggested, "Let Maggie tell us." From then on, testing dogs for cat compatibility was her job.

Every day Maggie bravely sits on a table in the volunteer center while the staff brings in one leashed dog at a time and watches its reaction. If the dog ignores or politely sniffs Maggie, it's proven to be adoptable in homes with cats. But if it barks or lunges at her, the dog goes to a cat-free family. With unruly dogs, Maggie arches her back and fluffs out her fur to look bigger. She growls, hisses, and bravely holds her ground. She once flew across the table at a hostile dalmation. After those tests which seem to jangle her nerves, Maggie wanders off alone to rest. The staff respects the cat's wish for a time-out.

For the past nine years, Maggie has confronted two or three dogs every day. This isn't the most stress-free life for a feline, but by willingly facing danger that she's well aware of, Maggie may have saved hundreds of family cats from injury or death. Says Liz Baronowski, the shelter's director of humane education, "Her work is one little step, but it's such an important one." Maggie's job requires daily courage.

Souvenir, a black Lab, also needed courage for his even more dangerous work detecting explosives. Originally trained as a disabled person's service dog, Souvenir tended to growl too aggressively at other dogs and so was turned over to the California Highway Patrol, where he was trained on protective detail. At the command "seek," Souvenir would sniff for dynamite, TNT, black powder, detonating cords, and other bomb materials. To signal the location of explosives, he'd sit down immediately when he found them and look at his handler, Doug Green.

From his very first lesson in bomb sniffing, Souvenir took the job extremely seriously. He was usually an easygoing dog who let babies crawl all over him, but, says Green, "at work his personality changed. He was intense and focused, like he had a job to do, and nothing was going to stop him. He showed that kind of determination."

Soon after Souvenir started his career, Green left him in his van while he detonated dynamite at a police officers' training demonstration. At the blast, Souvenir, who'd never heard an explosion before, vomited in terror. Later, as he got more experienced, he understood that someone shouting "fire in the hole" meant that an explosion was coming. Yet each time he heard the warning, he would lean against Green's legs for reassurance.

Apparently, familiarity with bombs did not take away the dog's natural fear of them.

Did Souvenir associate those frightening blasts with the bombs he was so often asked to find? "It's highly probable," Green says. "To get the explosives to where we'd detonate them in demonstrations, we had to carry them in the van. Souvenir would smell them there. He put the smell together with the future explosion."

Nevertheless, for eight years Souvenir bravely went after bombs in schools, hotels, airports, offices, and stadiums. He protected Presidents Ford, Carter, Reagan, and Clinton, and he once found a bomb sent by mail to California Governor Pete Wilson. This dog helped thousands of people. Says Green, "Souvenir knew there was danger, but he completed the job every time."

Animal courage isn't always as dramatic or fraught with extreme danger as the stories of Brandy and Souvenir demonstrate. Sometimes, the bravery is subtle and long term, when an animal suffers difficulties or anxiety without complaint day after day, sometimes for months or years. This kind of courage is quiet and easily unnoticed, the kind shown by experimental animals who live dismal lives in cages. In some ways, however, this courage of endurance can seem even greater than those brave acts that make headlines.

One animal who showed rugged, long-lasting courage was Orient, a German shepherd seeing-eye dog. For eight and a half months, Orient guided Bill Irwin, blind from a degenerative disease, along the Appalachian Trail. This was no short, leisurely hike: The journey started in Georgia and ended in Maine—and went on and on for 2,168 often extremely challenging miles. Some people may have felt it was cruel of Irwin to take a dog on such a long and difficult trip, but Orient bravely kept going in spite of what must have seemed to him in the beginning like endless hardship.

As the trip progressed, the dog's courage grew. Before starting down the Appalachian Trail, Orient had never walked on a surface other than concrete; now he suddenly was in the wilderness. Trained to stop at every elevation and depression of more than an inch and a half, he found himself surrounded by rocks and holes of that size and larger. He didn't know what to do, recalls Irwin. And Orient also didn't know how to take care of Irwin at the start of the trip when his guardian would crash to the ground hundreds of times every day. Orient had to learn quickly how to guide in this new, extremely stressful situation. "It took courage for him to be willing to work like that," Irwin says.

For the dog, overcoming physical limitations took courage, too. For sixteen hours a day, Orient had to work. At the beginning of the journey, he would get so tired trying to do what Irwin wanted that he constantly had to stop and rest. By evening he'd be too exhausted even to raise his head to eat, and would go hungry. In the mornings when Irwin picked up Orient's halter and backpack, the dog would hide in a corner of their shelter to avoid another overwhelming day. But slowly, even though Orient had to go against his basic physical nature, he bravely adapted and built endurance.

Orient's backpack didn't work well with his harness, yet he kept going mile after mile, even as straps carved lesions down to the muscles behind his front legs. Sharp rocks cut his tender feet. Even so, says Irwin, "Orient was willing to continue on, to persevere. He had the courage to live with pain."

And with discomfort. One morning when Irwin woke, he found Orient still sleeping, covered with snow. On another day,

Irwin ran out of water, and Orient was so thirsty that he lifted his head to drink rain. In spite of his daily nine thousand calorie diet, the dog sometimes lost weight. Still, he bravely endured all the physical hardships. As the months wore on, Orient led Irwin through heat, rain, bitter cold, fierce winds, and snowstorms.

Once he became physically strong and learned how to guide Irwin in the wilderness, he seemed to love the adventure. He figured out how to read trail markers to keep Irwin on course and could lead his guardian for a mile along an eight-inch trail with a two thousand foot drop on either side. On vertical climbs up sheer rock faces, Irwin lifted Orient under his haunches, and the brave dog would dig his toenails into whatever he could reach to scramble higher. Orient and Irwin swam through thirty-five-mile-an-hour currents to cross a river. They met bears, snakes, deer, and people. Instead of constantly having to muster courage as they'd done at the start of the trip, Orient and Irwin enjoyed themselves.

Another quietly courageous dog was Michael, a nearly albino collie with a few patches of salt-and-pepper in his shaggy white fur. His life was the opposite of Orient's because Michael was blind and deaf, and he needed his guardian, Ruth Hankins, to guide and protect *him*. Many of us would find Michael's physical and emotional burdens overwhelming if we had the same disabilities. His bravery was all about finding pleasure in spite of them, persevering and living gracefully with severe and surely sometimes frightening limitations.

The first time Hankins saw Michael, she thought he looked like a baby piglet with small eyes, a long snout, and pink skin that showed through his white fur. She remembers that he walked fearlessly up to her and sniffed her. "With his disabilities, you'd think he'd have been shy and cowering," Hankins says, "but that wasn't the case at all."

After she brought him home to Woodbury, New Jersey,

Hankins first had to teach Michael how to go up and down steps. On one of his first trips down, while she was distracted for an instant, he fell, spread-eagle, to the landing. From then on, Michael never again tried to negotiate stairs without her guidance. Hankins would stand in front of him, take his front paws, and place them on the next step he should take. Then she'd hold Michael's head, and he'd know to follow.

Hankins decided that, at age two, Michael needed exercise. Though she was apprehensive, she took him for a walk. At the first curb, she pulled up on Michael's leash and without understanding what she was trying to convey, the dog stepped forward and stumbled. On the curb across the street, she pulled his leash up again, and he knew immediately that he was approaching a step. Hankins later adjusted her tugging—the harder she pulled, the higher the step that was coming. With only his nose to give him clues to his surroundings, Michael bravely adapted to taking walks, and he accepted the curious sniffs of strange dogs he could not see or hear.

One of these was a hyperactive dalmation who had come to live in Hankins's house. For weeks, Michael tolerated the other dog's constant nips and paws placed on his shoulders to prove dominance. Then one day Michael had enough. Snarling and flashing his teeth, he slammed the dalmation against a bookcase, then stepped back and went his way. Fighting an unseen and unheard opponent took courage. Michael emerged as the alpha dog.

His bravery was readily apparent in his willingness to trust and, like Helen Keller, to eagerly meet what life sent without cowering at challenges. Late one night, for example, Hankins left Michael alone for a moment in her front yard without realizing that the gate was unlatched. The dog nosed it open and struck out alone for a walk.

With her heart in her throat, Hankins set out in search of Michael. Calling was no use; he could not hear her. So she walked, ran, looked down streets, and prayed the dog was safe. She imagined him falling into a hole or wandering into a wall; being picked up by a cruel stranger; or getting hit by a car he couldn't know was speeding toward him. Michael was defenseless, or so Hankins thought until she finally found him at the end of an alley, where he was ambling around, sniffing the concrete, confidently enjoying his adventure.

"Michael taught me courage because he lived it," Hankins says. "Whenever I felt sorry for him, he showed me with his grace and confidence that he was not a poor, pitiful dog." Michael taught Hankins that he did not have so many disabilities as she thought he had. His main limitation, in fact, often turned out to be her limited expectations of him. "Michael's strength made up for my weakness," Hankins says. "Courage was in his spirit."

Courage is in the spirit of so many animals, whether they're protecting us, working for us, or showing us by example how to endure hardship. When I think about how frightening life can sometimes be for animals, I have to appreciate how they can so bravely handle what comes at them. And so much of their courage is for our sake. We owe them a debt of gratitude.

4.

LOYALTY

Tari Hanes used to be an animal control officer at the Glad-stone Animal Shelter in Gladstone, Missouri. After nearly four years of working to improve the lives of dogs and cats by rounding them up and trying to find homes for them, she finally had to quit her job. When she explained why, she said, "I hope you have your tissues handy." I didn't, but I soon wished I did.

Two dogs, whom the shelter staff named Mr. and Mrs. Husky-Mix, had been picked up off the streets together. They were so obviously devoted to each other that every effort was made to find a home where both of them could live. One day during a regularly scheduled exercise period, Mr. Husky-Mix jumped the six-foot chain-link fence around the shelter's yard and escaped, but Mrs. Husky-Mix was too chubby to follow. So to keep from being separated from her, he came back and sat at the shelter door until a shelter worker let him back inside. Says Hanes, "He wanted to be with her more than he wanted to be free."

A month and a half later, no one had adopted the dogs, and with immense sadness, Hanes had to euthanize them. Together.

If Mr. Husky-Mix had kept running when he got outside the fence—and had not come back—he'd have still been alive. The poignancy of Mr. Husky-Mix's decision to remain with his mate gnawed at Hanes.

Then there was the case of two little yellow Lab mix brothers, just pups, who stayed for weeks at the shelter, unclaimed and unwanted. They seemed to adore each other: always romping and playing together and cuddling up into a pile to sleep. Their devotion was intense and unwavering. But no one took the pups home, and the wrenching time came for Hanes to put them down. After one pup had died, she gave the second an injection. Gathering his last bit of strength, he staggered to his brother and fell down beside him. With a lump in her throat, Hanes watched as he died, his head nestled on his beloved brother's back.

Not long afterward, a woman came into the shelter and asked the staff to find a new home for her thirteen-year-old beagle mix, Calamity. "When I saw this dog, my heart sank," Hanes remembers. "After you've worked in animal control for a while, you just know when a situation is not going to work out for the good of the pet"—especially an elderly animal, whom few people would be eager to adopt.

But Calamity's age turned out not to be the problem. It was Calamity herself. Ignoring the activity of the animals and people around her, she'd lie on her bed in the shelter's office and refuse even a bite of food. The staff assumed she was just having trouble adjusting to her new surroundings, and, to entice her to eat, they added canned food to her regular diet of dry kibble. But she'd just sniff at the meal and turn away.

On the third day after her arrival, the shelter staff gave Calamity cat food, which is ambrosia to most dogs. But the beagle wanted none of it. Thinking that she was perhaps used to table scraps, a staffer tried to tempt her with leftover pot roast with gravy from home. Another staffer brought the dog a McDonald's cheeseburger; but, though beagles are notorious for being portly dogs with voracious appetites, Calamity refused even a nibble of the delicious treats. Instead, she lay on her bed in a cloud of gloom.

Calamity got weak. Then weaker. In only days, she seemed to age ten years. Finally, one afternoon she got up from her bed, started across the room, and collapsed. Hanes picked her up and, with tears in her eyes, knew the time had come for an injection to end the animal's misery. "I think Calamity just grieved herself to death," Hanes said afterward. Abandonment by the guardian she loved was apparently more than Calamity could bear.

All these stories of animals at the Gladstone shelter are heartrending examples of a virtue *un*rewarded. The virtue these animals demonstrated was loyalty, also called constancy or steadfastness in affection and allegiance. Whatever the word, animals often choose to make beautiful attachments to us and to each other, attachments made evident by their attitude and actions and willingness to be faithful through thick or thin, for life. Animals are often more loyal than we are. They can choose to bond like glue.

When there is a tie between biologically unrelated animals, some researchers even go so far as to give the bond the human term "friendship." Beyond the anecdotal evidence of animal loyalty, there have been documented surveys that provide evidence of a willingness—even an eagerness—in animals of many species to be friends to others.

For example, Jon Pierce and his colleagues at Cambridge University found that sheep, given the choice between members of their own flock and sheep they didn't know, would run faithfully to their friends, whom they recognized by their horns and faces. German scientists Viktor and Annie Reinhardt discovered loyal ties in a semi-wild cattle herd. In addition to noting bonds formed between siblings, and between mothers and babies, the researchers saw that unrelated cows would become attached to each other. They showed their allegiance by grazing together and grooming each other.

Animals are usually most loyal to others of a similar species, rank, or age. Humans are the same: We often gravitate toward people who have a similar cultural background, who share our likes and dislikes, or who are going through important life stages at the same time we are and, therefore, share our interests. But we sometimes also grow close to others with whom we have little in common. Similarly, animals can reach across the boundaries between species to form odd, yet remarkably loyal attachments.

Koko, the famous hand-signing gorilla, faithfully befriended a kitten. A monkey from Bangladesh once adopted a puppy. At a South African wildlife rehabilitation center for orphaned primates, two infant baboons, named Holly and Berry, became so staunchly attached to adult Irish wolfhounds that they would curl up and fall asleep while resting their heads on the dogs' stomachs.

Diamond Dreamer, a black Lab mix from Margaretville, New York, became a loyal friend to a rabbit, Junior Bear, to whom Diamond plastered herself at every opportunity. The rabbit got a fungus and lost much of his fur, but Diamond cleaned him with her tongue and nursed him until he healed. Just as faithful was Samson, a huge, hundred-pound St. Bernard-rottweiler mix from Oshkosh, Wisconsin. The dog would lie in the sun for hours nuzzling Baby, his tiny, two-pound kitten friend. A neighbor's dog once charged into the yard to get her, and Samson crouched down over her to protect her. A few weeks later, he did the same when a hawk swooped down from a tree to snatch her away. Samson was loyally devoted.

Birds, perhaps surprisingly to some, can also form steadfast connections to animals of a vastly different species—even predators. Animal rights activist Karen Davis took note of a prairie chicken, who would sit every day on a branch beside an iguana she seemed to have befriended. Davis also described to me a rooster who would nap, side by side with a feline companion, and a bantam hen, named Jubilee, who often groomed the fur of her friend, an Australian sheep dog, and nestled next to him for hours.

An angora goat on a Fort Worth, Texas ranch, once demonstrated a deep loyalty to a feral cat. One cold, rainy winter afternoon, Kay Hollingsworth went out to feed the goat, named Nancy, her daily grain. But Nancy was not waiting, hungry and eager for dinner as usual. Though sometimes she'd been so voracious that she'd knocked the oat pan out of Hollingsworth's hands, on that day Hollingsworth found her lying in a kennel with the feral cat's babies, their eyes still closed, snuggled in her long, soft fur. Whenever the mother cat went hunting, the goat would babysit. Together, they created an odd but faithful two-species family.

Nancy

Romeo, a white rat, and Cinnamon, a German shepherd, developed a similar relationship. In *The Arizona Republic*, Kenneth White, executive director of the Arizona Humane Society, describes how Cinnamon would affectionately lick Romeo until he shone as if lacquered. The rat would travel all over the house on Cinnamon's back with his tiny front feet resting on her head. Cinnamon figured out how to nose open the latch of Romeo's cage and let the rat climb out. They would spend hours sleeping together, with the rat curled into a ball in Cinnamon's fur.

Sadly, Romeo died in just that position, and Cinnamon seemed to know the instant it happened. Careful not to shift positions and jostle the rat, Cinnamon moaned to call her human family. Cinnamon was devastated at Romeo's death, and for a week she sat in front of Romeo's empty cage and stared at it with sorrowful eyes. Just months later, ever faithful to her friend, the dog also died.

In cases demonstrating animal loyalty across species, something special is going on. The animals involved are making a somewhat anti-instinctive stretch in order to get so close to each other. They are also showing a tolerance for differences, an acceptance of others just as they are, and a willingness to lay aside natural animosities or fears. There's a beautiful trust involved in animal loyalty.

When bonds of loyalty develop between people and animals usually found in the wild, in particular, trust is a crucial factor. In *The Bears and I*, Robert Leslie describes rearing three black bear cubs in Canada. He had planned to teach them how to survive and then release them into their natural habitat, but unexpected emotions cropped up inside him when it was time to say goodbye. Leslie had no idea how close he would become to the bears and how loyal they would be to him. "I had felt sorry for three cute little teddy bear orphans, offered them temporary food and protection, trained them to meet their own responsibilities," he writes. "Then, out of the finest kind of obedience, respect, trust, compatibility, and affection, there had grown a depth of mutual friendship far beyond anything I could have believed possible at the time the cubs arrived."

For the bears' own good, however, the bonds had to be severed. When the last cub, Scratch, reached four hundred pounds and was too big to keep any longer, Leslie knew he had to return the bear to the wilderness. His friend Mark would transport Scratch two hundred miles by boat to his new home, and Leslie would see them off in his canoe.

At the moment of parting, Scratch, sitting in the bow of Mark's boat, must have seen the tears running down Leslie's cheeks, and as Leslie began to paddle south, Scratch understood that Leslie was leaving him. The bear loyally bounded over the side of Mark's launch to swim to Leslie.

Realizing that the only way to get Scratch to go out on his own was to make him feel that Leslie no longer cared about him, Leslie had to push him away. He struck him across the nose with a willow switch—the nose, Leslie writes that had "so often nudged me with affection and admiration." Scratch eventually swam back to Mark and climbed into the launch as Leslie paddled south. "Had I ever looked back," Leslie recalled, "I would never have left." Surely Scratch felt just as overwhelmed by the breaking of their loyal bond.

In *The Cheetahs of De Wildt*, Ann Van Dyk tells another story of loyalty, this one between her and Tana, a cheetah in her South African wildlife sanctuary, where Van Dyk breeds the animals to keep them from extinction. Whenever Van Dyk would walk by Tana, the cheetah pounced, affectionately nipping the back of Van Dyk's neck and purring with great devotion. They would often sit watching sunsets together, with Tana's head on Van Dyk's lap and Tana's rough, wet tongue on Van Dyk's hand to request stroking. This loyal friendship continued for years. Writes Van Dyk, "It is difficult to describe what it's like to experience trust and to receive such warmth and gentleness from a wild creature."

When Tana got injured, Van Dyk had to leave her to heal

with a vet at a nearby zoo. While away from Van Dyk, the cheetah pined and refused to eat; so to encourage her, Van Dyk paid
her a visit. She was shattered to see Tana lying on the floor,
unable to lift her head, her eyes barely open. Sure that the cheetah was dying, Van Dyk brought her home and slept beside her
to comfort her.

The next morning, Tana woke Van Dyk with a sharp cry. Her
breathing was labored, and her limbs were cold. After lifting her
head just enough to look into Van Dyk's eyes one last time, Tana
closed her eyes and died. Van Dyk saw that tears were streaming
down the black lines on the cheetah's face. The end of the loyal
friendship had been wrenching to them both.

All these stories show us clear examples of animals' intensely
faithful connections, but it's still a mystery what prompts
the creatures to act as they do. The truth is, the driving force
behind loyalty in animals is probably just as complicated as
human motivations for bonding.

In some cases, faithfulness may be attributed to hormones, as
University of Maryland researcher Sue Carter discovered in her
studies of prairie voles. Prairie voles are monogamous, as are
only three percent of all mammal species. Carter's studies have
shown that oxytocin, a hormone released from either the poste-
rior pituitary gland or the hypothalamus, may pave the way for
the rodents' permanent pair bonding. Usually prairie voles take
twenty-four hours to get to know each other before snuggling up
together, but after an injection of oxytocin, they start bonding in
fifteen minutes and seem to commit for good in only an hour.
Oxytocin is also connected to mothers of other species' attachment to their babies, and it is believed to play an important role

in establishing positive social interaction in humans and other animals. Oxytocin may be a basic building block of loyalty.

Scientists at Emory University's Yerkes Research Center have concluded that another hormone, vasopressin, released in male prairie voles when they mate, makes them faithfully bond with a female, guard her, and act paternally toward their baby prairie voles. Vasopressin is known to play a role in the general social behavior of males of many species. Sometimes called the social hormone, vasopressin is believed to influence animals to develop allegiances.

In addition to hormonal motivations, loyalty among animals may arise from a desire to benefit from the give-and-take support of a close relationship—support perhaps connected to the mutualism and reciprocal altruism that many experts feel negate true animal compassion. "Friendships are formed for advantage," says Sally Mendoza, psychology chair at the University of California at Davis. She studies titi monkeys, who often follow each other closely and eat and sleep together. By doing so, Mendoza believes, "they're less subject to predation and more likely to find food. They form friendships for their own good"—just as people sometimes do.

While observing new mother baboons on Botswana's Okovango Delta, University of Pennsylvania researcher Ryne Palombit saw that each mother would remain physically close to a male she'd mated with before her baby's birth. The female would follow the male, groom him, and invest time and energy in what seemed like a loyal relationship.

If her baby died, however, the mother would instantly lose interest in the male. Palombit's conclusion was that the female would encourage a bond in order to get the male's protection, since male baboons kill thirty-eight percent of babies in order to stop the mother's lactating and promote her ovulating, so she can conceive offspring with them. The mother's seeming loyalty to her male protector, Palombit decided, was basically for personal advantage. True constancy was nowhere to be seen.

Similarly, when watching young adult, subordinate male rats initiate play with a dominant rat, one might be tempted to see the hopeful stirrings of a loyal friendship. But according to Sergio Pellis, a psychology and neuroscience professor at the University of Lethbridge in Alberta, Canada, this friendship has nothing to do with trying to build a steadfast relationship. Pellis noted that the subordinate beta rat would rub his snout into the back of the alpha male's neck and nuzzle in order to get a play fight going. The beta was more likely to approach the alpha in this way than a fellow beta, and he would initiate the fun with the alpha far more often than the alpha did with him.

Pellis concluded that this was the beta's means of keeping on good terms with the alpha, so that the beta could stay close to the group's food source and its females. "The play keeps the friendship going," Pellis explained. "The beta is happy to hang around and get the crumbs." Those male betas may well be little sycophants, manipulating for their own good.

But just as often as we humans make superficial friendships for personal benefit, we can also be steadfastly connected to others and care deeply for them. It seems to me that animals are no different. Genuine emotion and good-heartedness can drive true loyalty in all species, and it certainly seemed to drive the faithfulness of another rat, named Annie. If we were to pit Annie against those beta males, her loyalty would shine as silver against their tin.

One day Annie was lying in her wood shavings and looking so obviously bored and depressed that her guardians, Elaine and Chuck Sandrell of St. Louis, Missouri, brought home another rat, Mollie, to be her companion. Almost immediately, the two rats began romping and playing and sleeping in a ball together. Their bond seemed closer than friendship; they acted like devoted sisters.

One afternoon Elaine and Chuck heard squeaking and mewling and rushed to the rats' cage. Mollie, they discovered, had been pregnant when they'd bought her, and she'd just given birth. But now she was hemorrhaging and clearly suffering. Annie, looking distressed, was right beside her. In fact, she may well have cried out specifically to get Elaine and Chuck to come and help.

With her nose and paws, Annie pushed a tiny baby against Mollie's stomach, where it could nurse. The baby survived in part because of Annie's help as a loyal and truly caring friend.

Pellis speculates that rats may get "warm fuzzies," just as we do, when they're near someone they like. Warmth and positive feeling is as far as he will go when theorizing on possible emotions behind animal friendship; but when I asked him if animals could be loyal, he replied, "The word describes a long-term process in which individuals stick by one another in times of adversity. At this descriptive level, there probably do exist cases in which non-human animal relationships may be described as loyal."

Pellis added, however, that when we apply the word "loyal" to a human relationship, we generally also incorporate the emotions and memories that lie behind the relationship. We might say, for instance, that we love or care about a person, or we might remember growing up with her or having a long, rich history as friends. "It is simply impossible to tell whether non-human animals have such cognitive content in their relationships," Pellis explains. "Our state of knowledge is too primitive to draw any meaningful conclusions." In other words, according to Pellis, we can't know whether Annie really cared about Mollie and whether she looked back on their pleasurable days of comradeship when she appeared to be so loyal by trying to help her and her baby.

Maybe we can't be sure how much animals actually think about their connection to others and what kind of memories and emotions they might bring to it to make it "loyal" in a human sense. In the end, however, those considerations seem far less important to me than do the beautiful actions that animals take. Animals can show what looks very much like unswerving allegiance to others, and behind it surely must lie intense feelings and a conscious choice.

I believe that, just as with humans, something good inside animals prompts their loyal behavior toward family and friends. Perhaps when they choose to be loyal, more than when they choose any other way of doing good, their action speaks louder than words.

I've collected literally hundreds of stories of animals loyally standing by humans in tough times. There seem to be three primary ways in which animals do this: warning of trouble, getting help, and offering help.

When animals faithfully warn us of trouble, it's often not just so we can get them out of it. Once when I was out of town, my German shepherd, Noble, nudged my husband awake to let him know that water was flooding into our house. The worst thing that could have happened to Noble is that his paws might have gotten wet, so it wasn't for reasons of personal gain that he wanted my husband to know about the problem. Louie, a parrot from Delray Beach, Florida, may have had the same intention when he squawked and squawked to warn his guardian, Gail Ennis, that an alligator was passing by her window. Without

Louie, who was perfectly safe, Ennis wouldn't have already been dialing 9-1-1 when the alligator suddenly shoved through the screen door. Louie's faithful warning may have saved her life.

Steadfast dogs, cats, pet monkeys, birds, and even rabbits have been known to alert human friends to burglars and intruders. So did Wednesday, a jet-black feline, who had been rescued from the S.P.C.A. by Melissa Milich. In a *Newsweek* essay, she describes lying in bed one night and hearing the sound of scratching at the front door of her one-room bungalow in Los Angeles. A neighborhood cat was surely making the noise, she thought, because the scratching was so loud and constant.

Suddenly, Wednesday bolted from Milich's pillow, where she slept every night. The cat dashed in circles around the bed and refused to be soothed. The big, persistent cat Milich imagined at the front door kept scratching, nonstop—until, glancing through the window at the top of the door, Milich saw blond hair and a man's head bent down as he industriously tried to pick the lock. Milich screamed and the man ran. Wednesday had loyally done all she could in her cat way to let Milich know of the danger.

If a warning isn't effective, animals may show their faithfulness in adverse times by getting help. There are scores of stories of loyal dogs and cats leading adults to children who are lost, ill, or flailing for their lives in swimming pools and rivers. Or the animals have sought assistance for adults who have collapsed after seizures, heart attacks, and injuries from accidents. Pooch, from Gilmer, Texas, once raced to her guardian, Mrs. Pleas Fortune. The dog kept leaping high in the air and yelping at the top of each leap to get her guardian to come and help Mr. Pleas Fortune, who was pinned under his tractor.

In Shawnee, Kansas, Mike Glenn, was pinned, flat on his back, under his Oldsmobile after the jack slipped as he was changing a tire. He was helplessly trapped unless his wife came home or someone passed by and stopped to assist him. His English springer spaniel, Brandi, curled up beside him as if to offer comfort, and Glenn said, "Get me the phone, girl," even though he was certain she had no idea what he was asking. With his one free hand, he half-heartedly gestured to the phone on his porch.

Amazingly, Brandi trotted to the porch and grabbed the phone in her mouth. A hundred-foot cord enabled her to return to Glenn and drop the receiver beside him so that he was able to call for help.

Animals faithfully get help not just for people, but also for other animals. I've heard of dogs who go for help to pull their dog friends out of lakes and rivers, for example, or their cat friends out of clothes dryers. A loyal Pennsylvania cat named Tramp once led her human family to help her golden retriever companion, Lady, whose paw was caught in a steel trap. Smudge, an English cat, once meowed until her guardian followed her to Smudge's brother, who had been shut up for ten days under floorboards in a nearby house under construction.

At South Africa's Wildcare, a baby elephant screamed and trumpeted in the middle of the night to get someone to come to assist her friend. They'd just been rescued together after the rest of their herd had been gunned down, and the staff found the distressed baby, standing with her trunk extended through her enclosure's bars, faithfully trying to caress her herdmate who'd just collapsed from trauma and exhaustion.

In Brownwood, Texas, as Glynn Franklin drove down a highway late one cold Christmas night, a horse suddenly appeared in his headlights. In obvious danger of getting hit, he stood, neighing and whinnying in the middle of four lanes of traffic. Franklin stopped and tried to get a rope around the horse's neck to lead him off the pavement, but every time Franklin got close, the horse moved a few feet out of reach. "He kept leading *me*," Franklin remembers. "I couldn't catch him."

Franklin called the police from a phone booth, and the horse then led him and an officer down a creek bank, where they found a female horse trapped in the brush. Franklin and the policeman cut her loose, and the male horse stood by in silence, looking immensely relieved. It was later determined that the female lived on the same ranch as the male and was his good friend. "He wouldn't have led us to her if he wasn't so loyal," Franklin says.

Animals' loyalty is evident whether they try to get help or actually jump right into a difficult situation and offer help themselves. I've heard of so many incidents in which animals have steadfastly stood by others in a time of adversity and given their all to get human and animal friends out of trouble.

One such animal was a pig, named Pru. Pru was walking through a field on a South African farm with her guardian, Dee Jones, when Jones wandered off the path and got stuck in a bog. Wet and cold and terrified, she was sinking deeper and deeper into the mud, so she threw a rope over Pru's neck. Understanding exactly what was needed, the pig put her head down and, with all her might, loyally tugged Jones from the mire.

Albert Hughes, a road foreman, was driving his truck through a road-widening project in Bedminster, Pennsylvania, when he came to an intersection and slammed on his brakes. In the middle of the road lay a baby. A German shepherd was frantically circling around the child to protect him from oncoming cars. Hughes got out and picked up the baby, and the loyal dog led him to the toddler's negligent (not so loyal) father.

When Greg Masters, a veterinarian, was motoring across a shipping channel near the Sunshine Skyway bridge in Tampa, Florida, he saw a dark shape bobbing motionless in the water. It was a dog, floating on her side, he realized. Masters was sure she was dead, but he came closer and saw her kick her hind leg. He pulled Shasta, a rottweiler, into his boat.

Badly bruised, Shasta was suffering from hypothermia and mild shock and had sustained nerve damage to her front paw. But her injuries were slight if you consider how she'd gotten them. She'd jumped from the 192-foot bridge. That's the equivalent of leaping off a sixteen-story building.

That morning, Shasta's guardian, John Radd, had jumped from the bridge and killed himself. His father was sure his son went first, and Shasta loyally followed. While no one can know whether she simply wanted to stay close to Radd or, more likely, was trying to save him, Radd's father points out that Shasta had always gone everywhere with his son. If she'd thought he needed help, she'd have faithfully given her life to provide it—as, in fact, she almost did.

In addition to stories of animals loyally rescuing humans, there are many examples of animals who try to save or comfort other animals, especially one they care about who is sick or injured. My very favorite was a stray dog, who can tell us everything we need to know about animal faithfulness. He was observed in Detroit by Sister Virginia Parker, who was driving home one night when she spotted him and his female companion. They were a pair of scrawny, starving strays, a collie and a German shepherd, traveling side by side along the road. Parker stopped to offer them water and kibble, which she carries in her car for just such occasions.

The dogs gulped down the kibble (and politely shared it with each other). The shepherd finished her half, then walked a few steps away while the collie continued eating. Suddenly, a speeding driver hit the shepherd with a hideous thump. She staggered a few yards and collapsed to the ground. The collie left his food and dashed to her and licked her face as she lay dying. "It was so beautiful that he would console her," says Sister Virginia. And so loyal.

R esearchers have forced animals to show their loyalty all too clearly in ghastly experiments, in which the animals are separated from their mothers, mates, and friends. The effect of such losses, the experiments show, can be as powerful and traumatic in animals as one would expect it to be in people. Primates, for instance, go into what's euphemistically called a protest/despair response: They get agitated, move around restlessly, and moan and shriek in distress. Eventually, they huddle down and withdraw, grieving and despondent.

Their distress can have significant physical affects: Researchers have shown that the loss of someone an animal is faithfully attached to can cause neurobiological changes in its body. For example, on the first night after a group of baby pigtail macaques were wrenched from their mothers, the babies sank into depression, and their body temperature and heart rate dropped. They demonstrated increased evidence of heart arrythmias and sleep disturbances. Once reunited with their mothers, thus restoring the faithful bond, this process was reversed.

Psychologist Sally Mendoza has found that when titi monkeys are taken from parents or mates, adrenaline rushes through the monkeys' bodies and gears them up for fight or flight. "They perceive separation as a threat, like when they're defending themselves," Mendoza explains. The adrenaline rush suggests that having loyal ties broken may be as distressing to these animals as confronting dangerous predators.

The separation also causes a release of the hormone cortisol, Mendoza discovered. Cortisol increases carbohydrate metabolism and gives the titi monkeys more energy, which enables them to search more vigorously for their parent or mate if they are living in the wild. Cortisol also eventually calms down the animals and shuts off the adrenal stress response to end the "frantic mode" they've been in. Cortisol might be acting to dampen the painful emotions behind the loss and severing of a faithful bond.

When loyal dogs get separated from people they are attached to, they go through the same physiological reactions as titi monkeys. In research at the Royal Veterinary and Agricultural University in Copenhagen, Jorgen Lund found that the barking and destructive behavior many dogs exhibit when their guardian leaves them are not necessarily caused by disobedience and boredom, as one might imagine. Rather, frustration and even fear set off the reaction, which is supposedly related to the dogs' dependency on the person who has left them.

Mendoza theorizes that dogs have been bred to have an exaggerated, prolonged attachment to humans, which may bring out their pained response. I'd say they also behave as they do because they love us and are loyal to us. When dogs are separated from us, their innate faithfulness can prompt their distress at our absence.

Dogs often show how loyal they are by what they do in order to be reunited with us. When separated from those they love, faithful dogs often go to desperate lengths to find them. Robbie, a police dog, was left in a New Orleans kennel while his handler went on vacation. The dog somehow worked open his kennel latch *and* a window and then, unswerving in his allegiance, he jumped out and ran to his handler's home.

Nicki, a faithful black-and-white mutt from Eagleville, Tennesee, once ran fifteen miles in pursuit of the school bus carrying his human family's youngest child. The dog sat patiently all day outside the child's kindergarten classroom. When school let out in the afternoon, Nicki chased the bus fifteen more miles back home again. He did this every Monday through Friday, rain or shine, for an entire school year.

Few dogs have put out as much effort to stay loyally close to someone as a springer spaniel named Teddy. Walking across an intersection in Halifax, Nova Scotia, Teddy and her guardian, John Munro, were hit by a car. Munro slid over the top of the vehicle's hood, crashed his head against the windshield, and was thrown into the air. He was still holding half of Teddy's broken leash while he lay, unconscious and gravely injured, on the sidewalk.

Teddy was probably dragged under the car for some distance since all the skin and fur were scraped off her paws. Although bleeding badly, and suffering from two broken front legs, Teddy faithfully pulled herself close to Munro, inch by agonizing inch. Munro found her cuddled into the space between his arm and body with her head resting on his chest. "She snapped at people who came to help me because she didn't want to be separated from me," Munro remembers.

Even a red Hereford bull showed loyalty by trying to stay with those he surely loved. Peanut, who lived on a ranch near Holiday, Florida, was put alone in a fenced pasture to keep him from interfering while his mates and their calves were loaded on a slaughter truck. But Peanut could still see what was happening to his friends and family, and he broke out of the gate and charged and gored a worker who was helping load the truck.

D eath is another form of separation that demonstrates the exquisite faithfulness of animals. After the death of someone they love, animals often grieve in a raw, basic, deeply emotional way that shows how aware of their loss the animals are and how greatly they value whoever has gone from them.

It's believed that some animals actually cry: A monkey was seen in Borneo with tears running down her cheeks. Loyally mourning animals pine and refuse to eat. They may carry their beloved dead around for days or have a ritual funeral in which they bury their dead. The *Irish Times* reported the story of a man who came upon a procession of weasels on a country road. Four at the front carried a weasel's dead body, as almost a hundred others in the pack walked along behind.

Female elephants—who live from birth to death in a herd with their mother, grandmother, sisters, aunts, and friends—tend to grow quiet and tense when they come to the body of a dead elephant. They smell it cautiously and seem to examine its skull, tusks, and bones with their trunks. It's thought that elephants may recognize the bones of dead relatives, and they may be showing faithfulness to them in this way.

Other loyal animals keep vigil over their dead loved ones. A mother moose will stay with her calf for hours, or even days, after it has died. Harp seal mothers have been photographed watching over the bodies of their babies, who were killed and skinned by hunters. In Madrid, a Lab-pointer mix planted himself outside the Gregorio Maranon Hospital emergency room for two months and mourned his guardian, who had died there.

In Canada, a Lab mix, named Makwa, tried to escape the pursuit of Royal Canadian Mounted Police in order to remain in the freezing cold and sleet besides Kokanne Lake. Five days earlier, his guardian Michael Trudeau, son of Canadian Prime Minister Pierre Trudeau, had been swept into the water by an avalanche. Rescuers had to physically haul Makwa away because he didn't want to leave the site or Michael's unrecovered body. Four months earlier, Michael himself had searched for days for Makwa, lost after an auto accident.

Cats, who are commonly thought to be independent and indifferent, can also be loyal vigil keepers. One may have been Bumper, a black-and-white cat from Portola Valley, California. (He got his name because he would often bump his head against the leg of his guardian, Virginia Burrill, to ask for petting.) When Burrill got sick, Bumper jumped on her bed and kept her constant company for the next four years until she died. Then her daughter moved the bed and rug out of the room. Every time she went back into it, however, Bumper was lying in the middle of the hardwood floor in the exact spot where her mother had lain in bed with him for so many years.

Animals will often keep loyal vigils at the place where those they love are buried. Stephanie Wolf, who rears orphaned primates in South Africa, had to have her dachshund, Toby, put down. Every morning for a month, Wolf's mongrel, Mandy, would lie on Toby's grave. Sometimes she took her ball and set it there, like an offering, before lying down and staring sadly for hours into space. The two had spent hours together, eating, sleeping, and running on the beach, and now, says Wolf, "It was as if Mandy was saying good-bye and trying to come to terms with Toby's death."

Spot, a Border collie from Macclesfield, England, was given to a new family after the death of his guardian, Denis Goodier. But Spot soon escaped from his new home. He traveled four miles to St. James Church, where officials found him, lying on Goodier's grave. No one can explain how he knew where to go or how he found his way. Experts theorize that Spot may have followed scents, but I prefer the local spiritual medium's explanation: The dog found the grave of his guardian by the power of love and loyalty.

Loyalty must surely account for the extreme grieving that animals sometimes do. In the absence of someone they love, they can be so devastated that they almost seem to will themselves to die. One such animal was Damani, a seventy-two-year-old elephant, who lived alone for five months at the Prince of Wales Zoo in Lucknow, India, before Champakali, a younger elephant, was brought to share her enclosure. Almost immediately the two became inseparable.

When Champakali gave birth to a stillborn calf and died, Damani was seen shedding real tears. She barely nibbled at the sugarcane, grass, and bananas, with which the staff tried to tempt her. Soon she quit eating altogether, and, in spite of 116-degree heat, she quit drinking water.

Though the zoo staff cooled her with water spray and fans and veterinarians gave her over twenty-five gallons of intravenous glucose, saline, and vitamins, none of the heroics worked. Damani rolled on her side and lay staring into space with sad, moist eyes, and then she died. The loyal old elephant may have been so overtaken by grief for her friend that she was determined to end her own life.

Griz, a captive grizzly bear, also seemed to will himself to die out of loyalty. After a train killed his mother, he was taken to live at Wildlife Images Rehabilitation and Education Center in Grants Pass, Oregon. One day a tiny, starving, stray tabby kitten wandered into his enclosure. The center's founder, Dave Siddons, braced himself to watch Griz eat her for lunch, but, instead, the bear very gently dropped small, bite-sized pieces of chicken in front of the animal.

The seven-hundred-pound bear and the kitten, who grew to a four-pound cat, became best friends. Griz shared his food, played with the cat, and cuddled her in his arms when they slept together. But one day she disappeared, and Griz was desolate. He lay around in misery for two months until he was found dead one morning. Some of the center's staff believe that Griz had died from a broken heart, which is perhaps the ultimate symbol of loyalty.

Jessica was an African hawk eagle, who was stolen from her nest as a fledgling. For some reason, she was passed from guardian to guardian almost as soon as she'd become attached to each one—more than twenty people in all. Her last guardian had locked her in a pitch-dark basement for eight months and fed her barely enough to keep her alive. Half crazed by this treatment, and by people's disloyalty to her, she once attacked a little boy, and his father tried to kick her to death.

All this cruelty had made her "insane, aggressive, and nasty," recalls Lorna Stanton, the founder of South Africa's Bateleur Raptor Rehabilitation Center, where Jessica finally ended up. When captive birds of prey imprint on a person, the loyalty goes beyond friendship and becomes as fierce as the birds themselves. Says Stanton, "They bond with you ten times stronger than love. And if you break the bond, it leaves the bird severely traumatized."

In fact, when Stanton once went away on a six-week trip, Jessica fell apart. She pulled out every one of her feathers that she could reach, so she looked, says Stanton, "like a chicken in a supermarket tray." From the cold, the newly bald Jessica contracted pneumonia. Staring into the distance with glazed eyes, she refused to touch her food. Stanton feels that the bird basically tried to commit suicide.

Though Jessica recovered after Stanton returned, she goes right back to grieving self-destruction if she sees Stanton so much as holding a suitcase or comes to believe for any other reason that she's leaving again. The loyal eagle seems unwilling— and even unable—to live without Stanton.

Jessica's loyalty has a twinge of neediness and vulnerability to it. But it's also proud and fierce and unyielding. That complex bundle of widely divergent emotion behind animal faithfulness is what makes it so interesting. It can draw out such a broad spectrum of freely chosen, sterling action.

Loyalty can make animals grieve and sacrifice and even die for others. It can also encourage them to offer favors, extend themselves, and be willing to look out for those to whom they are so bonded. And loyalty often brings out ferocious protectiveness as well as the gentlest comforting. All these actions tell us about animals' sensitivities, vulnerabilities, concerns, and devotion, and they show the emotional intensity that can lie behind animals' loyalty. Their faithfulness also makes clear their great capacity for love.

5.

FORTITUDE

Do animals have strength of character? When fate tests
them, do they choose to show their mettle? Instead of
whimpering and slinking away from the vicissitudes of life, do
animals meet them with backbone and determination?

The story of Justin, a bug-eyed King Charles spaniel, can
answer those questions. He was a tiny toy of a dog, the kind
who'd have snoozed royally on a silk pillow in a seventeenth-
century English court. Like those dogs, Justin was supremely
pampered. Now, in the autumn of his life, he had a heart murmur
and was deaf and delicate.

Nothing had prepared him for the odyssey that began when
guests of his guardian, Susan Warmflash, left open the front door
of her house. Justin sneaked outside and quickly got lost while
wandering his neighborhood in Closter, New Jersey. As he circled around to find his way back home again, he got more lost.

When Warmflash realized he'd disappeared, she searched
frantically for him. He undoubtedly searched for her, too, but
he wasn't able to hear her calling; and he must have been even
more disoriented by the cars that zoomed by too close, which he

couldn't hear either. Warmflash put up lost-dog posters, and one woman called to say she'd just seen Justin walking across a field near her house in pouring rain. "He looked really tired," the woman remarked. Warmflash rushed to find him, but the dog was gone.

Justin was lost all that summer. And fall. And most of the winter. Then finally, one icy February night—nine months after he'd disappeared—Justin dashed in front of a car traveling twenty miles from his home. The dog was so filthy that the driver barely saw him in the darkness, but the man jumped out of his car, caught Justin, and traced him to Warmflash by his rabies tag.

Justin had weathered downpours, heat, ice, and snow. As a cosseted family dog, suddenly alone and without the resources and love he'd been accustomed to, he faced the unknown every single day and was able to deal with supremely difficult challenges. Once used to curling up for leisurely naps on the sofa, he now had to scrounge for shelter. Used to hearty meals served in his bowl, he now had to forage for food. Used to petting and affection, Justin now had to cope with loneliness and despondency. Explains Warmflash, "He had to change his personality. He had to get fierce and strong and determined. He was just a tiny thing against the world."

Six months later, Warmflash still has to wake Justin very gently from his naps. She says, "If I touch him too hard, he startles terribly. Deep inside him, all the trauma is still there. He obviously went through really bad times." But once awake, Justin seems to put those times behind him. "It's taken strength for him to accept what happened to him," Warmflash adds. "He was a lot stronger than we thought."

Where do you think he got the strength to survive? I asked her.

"It was an inner strength. He may not have even realized he had it before he wandered off," Warmflash explains. "It's the same with us. We don't know about our strength until terrible things happen, and we have to pull it up and draw on it."

Instead of giving up and dying, Justin showed the grit of Goliath. When faced with disasters, emergencies, and problems often not of their own making, plenty of animals do the same. They pass muster in rough and trying circumstances, and they rise to difficult occasions. Animals' resilience, perseverance, and determination can be admirable. Animals can set worthy examples of fortitude for us.

Scientists easily acknowledge animals' physical strength, innate stamina, or genetically determined sturdiness, because weight, muscle mass, speed, and physical force can all be objectively measured. But animals' inner strength goes largely ignored because it has to do with an attitude that is subtle, subjective, not readily observable in laboratories, and normally used only to describe humans. Just because scientific experiments can't measure animals' fortitude, however, does not mean that they lack it. It's as evident in tiny, deaf Justin as in many other creatures and is as real as their breath or heartbeat.

Where the grit comes from is a matter of speculation. Animals may be born with a propensity for it, or they may develop it as they grow up and have their mettle tested. According to Michael Weiss, a veterinarian in Sewell, New Jersey, animals may learn to be strong by observing strength in others or by "seeing the good side of life," the side worth fighting for, he says. When animals have experienced love, comfort, or pleasure, they can draw on their knowledge of those things for the positive energy they need to fight to survive hard times.

And drawing on the knowledge may make animals determined to put those bad times behind them and return to their normal lives again. When animals are fighting illness, injury, loneliness, or any other kind of misery at veterinary clinics, for example, "their recovery process is driven by wanting to return from where they came," says Andrew Kallet, a veterinarian in Corte Madera, California. Animals want to go to the last place they experienced connection and well-being. Their eagerness may nurture their fortitude.

Whatever the source, Weiss says, "when animals show strength, I think it's a choice." Just as some people give up quickly in adversity while others have more drive to overcome it, some animals lie down and die in trying circumstances while others choose to show an incredible fighting spirit.

Animals may show even more fortitude than we do in a crisis, Kallet speculates, because we tend to worry about the future and become worn down by life's complexities and our own negativities. Those attitudes can become "layers of neuroses that are road blocks to our strength," Kallet believes. In contrast, animals may stay strong because they confront adversity without a human feeling of self-pity, and, says Kallet, "they accept their fate. What is, is what is. They live in the present. There's no forward projection of what the future might bring."

So often animals are determined fighters in adversity. They take no guff. They stand up sometimes to overwhelming difficulties and, with persistence and resilience, push to accomplish what they want.

All we have to do to see their inner strength is to look for the manifestations of it in their actions. In all the stories I've collected, I've found seven ways in which animals demonstrate fortitude:

The first of these is never giving up. Possibly even more than humans, animals can be tough and stubbornly determined to overcome adversity. In difficult situations, they often show their strength by their tenacity and demonstrate an amazing ability not just to survive but to endure.

My large file on trapped cats offers dozens of illustrations of this refusal to yield to misfortune. When accidentally confined, some of these cats did succumb and die, but others hung in without being defeated by their often hideous circumstances. I've heard of some cats who have waited for weeks before being rescued or having the chance to free themselves, and they needed more than physical strength or an instinctual drive for survival. Getting through the ordeal took grit.

One cat, Pinto, spent nineteen days inside the wall of a house under construction in Texas; another, Simon, lived twenty-two days caught under a box spring and packed in a crate on a moving van. Kate was closed up in a shipment of firebricks that traveled by sea for over a month from Belgium to Pittsburgh. Horace staggered out of a garage in Florida after having been accidentally locked inside for seven weeks.

Other indomitable cats have refused to give up when trapped in even more harrowing places, where strength of character must have been required as a means of fighting panic. One cat was Second Chance, who was handed over to a New York animal shelter in a box marked "poisoned by mistake." A pet cemetery's crematoria worker collected the box and found the cat inside, *alive*. Second Chance had not just survived ingesting poison. He had tenaciously held on while imprisoned for several days in the shelter's refrigerator.

Jacob, mascot cat of the *Tjoba*, was on the vessel when it sank on the Rhine River. Eight days later, cranes lifted up the wreckage from the riverbed, and the crew was allowed on board to salvage their belongings. When the captain opened his cabin door, out jumped Jacob, shivering and hungry, but not too bad for wear. He'd hung on for more than a week underwater, squeezed in a bubble of air.

Then there's Gus, a plump black-and-white cat from Ada, Michigan. His guardian, Diane Napierkowski, left her teenage son in charge of him last winter while she and her husband went out of town. Left outside, Gus curled up for warmth in a tiny space between a culvert and a knocked-down wall. While he slept, a blizzard covered his hiding place with snow. Then snowplows came through the neighborhood and piled on still more.

Nine days later, Napierkowski returned home and parked her van near where Gus was entombed in snow, unbeknownst to her. The noise of her unpacking drowned out his desperate meows. For days Napierkowski went out and called Gus, but a strong wind was blowing, and, she says, "it must have covered up the sound of his little cries." Finally, on a still, quiet afternoon, she and her son noticed a muffled meow coming from under the snow near the mailbox. They dug frantically with their hands until Gus's nose and whiskers emerged. Then he poked out his head and blinked in the sunlight. Weak, wobbly, and emaciated, but also clearly determined to live, Gus had been trapped under more than two feet of snow for sixteen days.

It's hard to imagine how Gus or any of these trapped cats endured their ordeals. As their stomachs growled and their mouths grew parched, they must have felt overwhelming discomfort, loneliness, helplessness, and terror. Yet they surely drew on inner strength and fought the physical hardship and emotional stress. Because Gus was still crying for help sixteen days after having been buried in snow, Napierkowski believes that "he kept reaching out and hoping and never giving up." That remarkable tenacity is an indication of this animal's fortitude.

Rupert, an African gray parrot—who got her name before

her guardian, Lynn Norley, realized that the bird was female—also showed inner strength by never giving up. She squawked one winter night to wake Norley to a fire, then gasped and went limp from heat and smoke inhalation. Thinking that the bird was dead, Norley wrapped her in a bathrobe and left her in the shower stall—the quickest "burial" Norley could arrange in the emergency. Then she climbed out the window to escape the flames. The next morning after the fire was extinguished, Norley dug Rupert out of a pile of soggy insulation, broken tiles, and burned wood. The bird was still alive.

Though her blackened feathers reeked of soot, Rupert had stubbornly survived fire, hosed water, burial under sodden debris on a freezing night, and abandonment. With that many physical and psychological strikes against her all at once, she surely needed moral strength to keep from buckling under and yielding to the crisis. A few days later, though, her breathing became labored and gurgly. Her eyes grew dull, and she stopped eating. Veterinarian Michael Weiss soon discovered that toxic fumes, heat, and then moisture had irritated Rupert's respiratory system, and aspergillus fungus was growing in her lungs.

For the next days, Rupert lived in an oxygen tank. She was force-fed through a tube to her stomach, had an endoscope pushed down her throat for a trachea exam, and had medicine squirted twice daily down her gullet. With such invasive treatment, says Weiss, "some birds give up. All of a sudden they just pack it in. But Rupert refused to do that. You could see fight in the bird. She had a tremendous will to live."

Late one afternoon at the end of her second week in Weiss's clinic, Rupert started to wheeze, then fell off her perch, unconscious. Weiss rushed to prepare for emergency surgery, but then Rupert suddenly came to. She brightly squawked, "Hi, ya, Rup!" as if to say, "Hi, everybody! Here I am! I'm fine!" Like a phoenix rising from an ash heap of adversity, Rupert soon was well enough to leave the clinic.

Weiss has various medical theories about how the bird managed to survive. Most important, he feels, was her unwillingness to balk at hardship or to fold under stress. "This bird seemed to have some type of special spirit, something you could sense," says Weiss. "Looking at her, you could almost see the strength."

In addition to refusing to give up, Rupert demonstrated an enormous reservoir of resilience, the second manifestation of animals' fortitude. Some animals will recover easily from disasters that one would expect to kill them or at least frighten them to death. When the creatures bounce back quickly, they show not just stamina, but also grit and a fighting spirit.

Again, cats can be extraordinary in this respect. Sometimes they seem to walk away from extreme hardship as if nothing had happened. Bobby, for example, fell asleep in the landing gear of a jumbo jet and traveled at thirty-five thousand feet—in freezing temperatures and with little oxygen—for seventeen hundred miles from Houston to New York. Apparently he was a bit shaken when he was discovered, but he traveled right back home in the cockpit and nonchalantly nibbled on an in-flight meal of poached salmon.

Hoover, a three-month-old kitten from Southington, Connecticut, got sucked—at 175 miles per hour—through the vacuum hose of a leaf-collecting truck. When highway workers looked in the truck's collection bin, they found the cat sitting on a pile of leaves. He was trembling but proved himself amazingly able to withstand the ordeal. Hoover resiliently recovered in minutes.

Easily weathering an even more traumatic experience was Sweet Pea, accidentally picked up in a Gillette, Wyoming dumpster and thrown into a garbage truck. Five or six times, a metal ram pressed all the garbage forward in the truck bed and compacted the garbage—*and* Sweet Pea, who got smashed flat against the refuse and had all the breath pushed out of her lungs. The garbage was dumped at a bailing station, and Sweet Pea landed at the bottom of the pile under at least a thousand pounds of trash. "It was like a person getting buried in an avalanche," recalls recycling coordinator Craig McOmie. "It would have been easy for her to lie there and die."

But Sweet Pea clawed her way to the top and popped out, dazed and howling, her usually immaculate fur spiked with rotting food. A few minutes later, one of the garbage collectors cleaned her up and drove her to a local animal shelter. As Sweet Pea rode along, she enjoyed a meal of cat food in the truck's cab. No one would have guessed what terror and suffering the amazingly resilient cat had just endured.

Another cat, Gros Minou, fell twenty stories—more than three hundred feet—but his only injury, a broken pelvis, quickly healed. Sparky, an English cat, got an eleven-thousand-volt shock but soon bounced back to health. Sam, a cat from Indiana, was sucked up into a tornado, whirled through the sky with flying debris, and dumped, severely injured, to the ground—but made a rapid recovery. Chrysallis, a stray cat from Ottawa, was hit by a car, then had to survive outdoors for a month in winter cold that sometimes reached minus-fifty degrees. A veterinarian had to wait two days for her to thaw out enough for him to gage her body temperature. After she warmed up, though, and her injured and frostbitten leg was amputated, she immediately purred and became rambunctious.

You might think, well, cats have nine lives and *should* be resilient after brushes with death. But other species of animals also display fortitude by easily recovering from devastating injuries. Sometimes, as those animals heal, they can show a third sign of strength: keeping up their spirits. Often when animals face hardship, they refuse to let it drag them down emotionally. Instead of doing the animal equivalent of giving in to depression, they seem to sustain a positive attitude.

I don't think I've ever heard of an animal who showed greater strength through high spirits than Rudy, a floppy-eared mutt, whose coloring and long legs hint of German shepherd ancestry. Just out of puppyhood, he took a walk in Mount Prospect, Illinois, with his guardian, Jenny Wendel. Rudy ran off after a flock of geese and was hit by a car. The speeding driver never even applied his brakes.

Rudy

Rudy's veterinarian shook his head in dismay at the dog, who was in shock and laboring to breathe on the examination table. Rudy's lungs had collapsed and his chest had filled with blood. He was in such bad shape, in fact, that the vet decided to see if the dog survived the night before conducting further diagnostic tests. "It's not looking good," the vet told Wendel, and she knew he was telling her to expect no miracles.

The next day, in spite of cracked ribs, internal injuries, a broken scapula, a badly mangled leg, and a severely damaged spine, Rudy held his own. When Wendel picked him up to take him to a spine specialist, Rudy managed to stand up and then limp happily to her. Acting carefree and cheerful, "he wagged his tail and gave me kisses," she says.

The spine specialist could not believe that Rudy was walking. Aside from having an unusable leg, the dog's back was broken, and he should have been paralyzed from his shoulders down. Surgery was done to put his spine together again with wires and pins. The very next day, in spite of pain and an eighteen-inch incision, Rudy, incredibly, was walking and in the highest spirits once again.

Once home, despite his slowly healing back and gimp leg, Wendel says, "Rudy was exuberant. He wanted to run and play." He kept catching his hurt leg on gates, fences, and chairs, though, so, six months later, the decision was made to amputate. On the very day after surgery, Rudy was psychologically "up" and ready to go. On three legs, he hobbled to Wendel, and he seemed never to look back for an instant at his loss or suffering.

"Rudy never complained or got depressed. After both his surgeries, there was a spark in his eyes, like 'I know something bad has happened, but I'm not going to let it get me down,'" Wendel says. She believes that Rudy was thinking something like, "Okay, I'm missing a leg. Life threw me a curve ball, but let's get on with it. I'll do the best I can with what I have."

After Wendel helped him climb stairs just a couple of times, he did it on his own. She put a dog life vest on him and let him swim; soon he paddled so well with just one front leg that he no longer needed the vest at all. Then he learned to run agility courses. Without a moment's hesitation, he'd go up ladders, down teeter-totters, over jumps, and through tunnels that required him to hunch down and crawl. Explains Wendel, "He dealt with his problems and moved on with a positive attitude."

Of course, some animals fall into depression in tough times. That emotion may be an exception, however, and Rudy's cheerful attitude may more likely be the rule. According to veterinarian Andrew Kallet, "Animals normally have the same state of mind every day, and it's outgoing and enthusiastic. They're upbeat and ready to go." We can't know whether animals' typical positive outlook is drawn from their inner strength or whether it fuels their will. But fortitude and optimism seem to go together in animals, just as in people. When animals show a positive spirit, they underscore how strong they are.

When animals choose to put adversity behind them, I believe that they show an animal version of forgiveness, the fourth sign of their strength. I'm not suggesting that animals go around, as we do, with the lofty thought that "to err is human; to forgive, divine." But they do show by their actions that they seem to accept what fate sends them, to let bygones be bygones, to rise above others' indifference, meanness, and even cruelty. When we make these attitude choices, we call it forgiveness. Why can't the same be said for animals? Whether one is human *or* animal, choosing to forgive and leave the painful past behind is no mean accomplishment. As we all know, it takes inner strength.

When animals are abused, but then pick up the pieces of their lives and bring themselves to trust people again, they show that they are titans of strength. One such animal was Electra, a scrawny, flea-infested, gray-and-white kitten, described in *Cat Fancy*. She was found hanging by her tiny hind legs from a string connected to a light switch. As she desperately struggled to free herself—turning the light off and on, off and on, in the process— her legs became red, raw, hugely swollen, and unspeakably painful. The veterinarian who treated her at California's Marin County Humane Society feared that hanging upside down for so long had permanently damaged nerves in her legs and brain.

The first time he reached into her cage, she hissed and spat and tried to claw him—a perfectly understandable response for a kitten who had so badly suffered. But he and the staff kept working to convince her that not all humans were brutes. Finally, one day, as a shelter employee held Electra in her arms, the kitten purred. That marked a cataclysmic shift in her attitude and the moment that she started to forgive.

A shelter supervisor eventually took Electra home, where daily physical therapy healed her legs, and constant attention apparently healed her fearful emotions. Soon with a sleek, healthy coat and new confidence, the cat accompanied the supervisor to work every day, where she'd lie close to her on a chair or window ledge. Despite such an abusive start in life, Electra chose to trust people. In her cat way, she mustered the grit to let go of past cruelty and trauma.

Monty, a white collie, marshaled his strength to leave behind equally traumatic origins. For his first three years of life, he was locked in a tiny cage outdoors at a Montana puppy mill, where he endured frequent beatings and freezing winter temperatures, and was given only rare drinks of water and barely enough food to survive. His day-to-day existence was one long, endless string of suffering. When a sheriff responding to animal cruelty complaints found Monty, the pitiful dog weighed just thirty pounds and was lying up to his hips in mud and feces. Once out of his cage, he did not know how to walk straight but moved only in the circles that he'd made all his life while confined.

Later, Irene Cohen saw him at a shelter. "He looked like he was in abject despair," she says. Feeling sorry for him, she adopted the dog, who trembled with fear in her car on their way to her home. When Monty was let out in the backyard, it became clear that he was terrified of grass, which he'd never walked on, and of Cohen and her husband, two more people whom he surely assumed would abuse him. Monty at first refused to come near them; but, finally, he gathered his strength and inched toward Cohen. Resting a paw on her shoulder, Monty started to overcome all the cruelty he had suffered.

Eventually, he figured out that the smell of hamburger being cooked in the kitchen meant delicious food, and his nervous stomach calmed. He stopped hiding under Cohen's desk or putting his head behind the sofa, like an ostrich trying to keep from being seen. He realized that being petted was enjoyable, and he often plastered himself to Cohen. Finally, he began to allow her houseguests to pet him, too. Explains Cohen, "Monty had the strength to allow himself to feel love and to forgive."

Sometimes, after surviving a living nightmare, animals will not only let go and forgive, but they also seem to grow in positive ways from the adversity, just as we often do. That growth from hardship is the fifth sign of animals' inner strength.

Lucky, a six-week-old calico kitten from Benton City, Washington, was the quintessential scaredy-cat. She was terrified of people, and one day, to get out of sight, she crawled under Becki Strader's Honda. The hiding spot she found was hardly comfortable. All that supported Lucky's body was a metal lip that curled back toward the car's bumper and formed a little ledge. It was too small for a resting place. To support her weight, the kitten had to crouch down and hang on.

Unaware that Lucky was hiding there, Strader started her car and headed for a wedding. Traveling down the freeway at seventy miles an hour, Lucky must have hung on with every bit of physical and emotional strength she could draw out of herself. For 200 miles—three long and surely almost unendurable hours—terrifying noises assaulted the kitten, wind blasted her face, and dirt spewed up from the asphalt and encrusted her fur. After Strader arrived at her destination, Lucky kept hanging on, all through the night and all the next day while the car was parked.

On the second night, Strader went outside to drive her car to a party. She heard a cat. "The sound was more than a meow. It was crying, like a cat was hurt," Strader remembers. When she looked for the source of the noise, she found Lucky. The kitten was filthy and "really shook up," Strader says. To calm Lucky down, she took her inside for a bowl of milk.

As soon as Lucky stopped crying, she seemed to leave her scaredy-cat days behind her. Apparently, her thirty-six hours of terror under the bumper had been some sort of kitten's trial by fire, from which she emerged strong and confident. "After going through all she did, she lost her fear of life and her fear of people," Strader says. "She wasn't afraid of anything." Lucky had passed a test of terrible adversity, and, showing admirable fortitude, she grew from the hardship.

The same could be said for an eagle named Osceola, whom I met in Tennessee on a writing assignment a few years ago. Though all eagles appear strong and powerful, those qualities seemed to emanate from this particular bird in a dazzling way. You'd never guess that he'd been through an arduous trial.

Probably using the eagle for target practice, someone had shot his wing. The bird was captured and turned over to John Stokes, then coordinator of the raptor rehabilitation program at the Memphis Zoo. Every effort was made to

Osceola

patch up Osceola, but one day Stokes found him with his eyes glazed and his feathers fluffed from fever, chills, and infection. The sorry time had come to amputate his wing.

Afterward, put in a large outdoor pen, Osceola would hop from the lowest to the highest perch and, determined to fly, would flap his good wing and his nub. Stokes lowered the perches to keep Osceola from getting high enough even to think about flying and possibly hurt himself from falling. Three months later, however, when Stokes put leather jesse straps on the eagle's legs and set him on his gloved hand, the fiercely persevering bird tried to fly—and fell—again.

As he slowly began to adjust to his fate as a captive bird, his grit became clearly apparent through a change in his behavior and attitude. He must have realized that his nub of a wing was never going to work, and he stopped trying to fly with it. He quit endlessly gazing up at the sky through the wire mesh that hemmed him in, and on his perch he waited—disabled, but dignified and patient—for dead mice and fish to be tossed to him. Rarely did he bite anyone in anger, as he'd done initially after his injury. His personal infinitive seemed to be "to accept." For all of us, animal and human, growing to accept what we don't like in life takes inner strength.

Osceola grew to participate in activities rarely expected of eagles. For example, when Stokes took him to schools for wildlife education programs, Osceola would emerge from his traveling cage to the excited screams of children, "thousands of a totally foreign species, all hollering at him," Stokes says. "He could have resisted or been afraid, but he adjusted. He'd flap his one wing for the kids without hanging back. He was confident and strong"—in a way he'd never have been in the wild.

Stokes, a hang glider, got the idea of taking Osceola up into the sky with him, so the eagle could experience flying again.

Stokes had a special harness made for the bird, and would at first hang him in it for thirty minutes at a time from a hook in a ceiling beam. When Osceola had become accustomed to the harness, Stokes attached the eagle to the wing of a glider and took him up in the air.

Having grown to accept the harness and his unnatural, sometimes bewildering situation, the eagle truly seemed to enjoy the flight. "There had to have been a lot of fear for Osceola to go into this new situation and to put up with so many new sets of variables," Stokes says. "But Osceola adjusted to everything. He lived up to what was asked of him. And growing like that took a lot of strength of character."

Wendy, a mare, showed strength by growing from adversity, too. Animal cruelty investigators found her, looking downtrodden and defeated, in a tiny pen adjoining a vacant house in Tinley Park, Illinois. A hideous, untreated wound on her leg indicated that she'd been used in rodeo horse-tripping events: At full gallop, a rider on another horse had chased her, lassooed her legs, and flipped her to the ground. After repeatedly enduring this cruel treatment, Wendy had sustained a wound that grew to a gaping, saucer-sized crater. Her pain must have been excruciating.

Wendy was turned over to the Hooved Animal Humane Society in Woodstock, Illinois. "At first she was terrified. She'd almost kick your head off," says Donna Ewing, the society's director. That was bad news because twice every day, hot compresses had to be applied to Wendy's wound, which also had to be scrubbed, treated with topical medications, and re-bandaged. At first, every treatment required wrestling and force, but after a few weeks Wendy trusted the shelter staff enough to allow them to attend to her. "Wendy became affectionate and bonded to people," explains Ewing.

Then Wendy got hit with another ordeal. While out on a ride, she severed a tendon and for the second time in her life could barely walk. She endured surgery, six weeks in a cast, and four in a hard splint. Then she had to spend fourteen more weeks confined to a narrow stall. Permanent resentment of everyone around her would have been understandable. But Wendy didn't seem to hold grudges.

Once her tendon healed and she was let outdoors again, she bucked and ran with what looked to Ewing like pure joy. It was the opposite of the desolation and anger that animal cruelty investigators had originally seen in her. Says Ewing, "Wendy redefined for the shelter staff the strong spirit of the horse." With that strong spirit, this animal had grown and changed from the hardship she endured.

A nimals can not only grow *from* adversity; they can be level-headed when they're in the *midst* of it. That calm in life's storms is their sixth sign of strength. When confusion swirls around them, they often keep going, sure and steady, depending on their strong common sense and self-possession. Driving this composure is their fortitude.

Probably the animal who showed the greatest composure in a crisis was Bill, an Australian blue heeler. While on a business trip to New York, his guardian, Jeth Weinrich, wrapped the dog's leash around a store doorknob and then went inside, assuming that Bill would wait for him, as always. But a security guard ran at Bill, and the dog, wary of strangers, pulled away and yanked loose his leash.

Bill ran away down the street. But even though New York City was a brutal and confusing place for a lost dog, especially one who had spent part of his life herding cattle on a peaceful, isolated ranch in Canada, Weinrich had faith that Bill would be all right. Once when he and Bill had gotten separated in Lyon, France, the dog had calmly swum across the Rhone River and found his way back to Weinrich's hotel. With Bill's grit and self-possession, Weinrich hoped, the dog would manage to return again this time.

Weinrich put up ten thousand fliers all over Manhattan and advertised a $5,000 reward in newspapers. TV stations started broadcasting updates, and Weinrich was avalanched with calls from people who'd spotted Bill. One person had grabbed the dog in Central Park—but Bill had tugged free and run on. Other callers had seen the dog sitting on the sidewalk just a block from Weinrich's hotel.

At one point, Weinrich learned that a dog, heading toward New Jersey in the Holland Tunnel, was blocking rush-hour traffic. The dog was Bill. To avoid police, who'd set up roadblocks to catch him, Bill turned around, avoided all the swerving tires, and ran back toward Manhattan. City trucks, with lights flashing and horns honking, came at him to frighten him back him toward the waiting police, and Bill obligingly reversed his course, but, says Weinrich, "You can't catch him if he doesn't want you to." Coping well with the duress, the dog wriggled through the policemen's legs and took off toward Hoboken, New Jersey.

A few days later, Bill must have realized he'd made a wrong turn and needed to get back to Manhattan. So he trotted toward the Holland Tunnel again. This time, onlookers claimed, a driver deliberately aimed at him and hit him. Bill and Weinrich were finally reunited at a Staten Island veterinary clinic, where the dog was diagnosed with compressed vertebrae and a bruised spinal cord.

Bill had kept himself safe for five days in terrible, chaotic conditions; and Weinrich believes that the dog was able to maintain his cool in traffic because, as a puppy, he'd learned to be extremely street-smart. "I never saw him walk on a road without looking to see if a car was coming," Weinrich says. And Bill has a steadiness about him. "His way of looking at the world is so solid. He's never reckless. His common sense is more than surface common sense. It's a deeper understanding," Weinrich adds.

That street-smart, levelheaded grasp of things is an indication, Weinrich believes, of "Bill's incredible strength and determination." And so was the dog's unrelenting purposefulness about making his way back to the hotel. "Bill was absolutely trying to find me. He was just trying to figure out how. He had a goal, a need. And once he's focused on something, he doesn't deviate from the path," Weinrich says.

That focus and determination is not unusual for animals. Staying the course to accomplish a mission is their seventh sign of strength. They most clearly show it, as Bill did, when they try to get to a place or a person. I've collected dozens of stories of animals who keep their attention riveted on the search, as if nothing could possibly stop them. Their force of will reveals much about their grit.

Sometimes, the animals just want to get home, as did Polly, a cow in England. She was sold to a farm two miles from where she'd always lived, and, just twenty-four hours later, she sneaked through a door left ajar in her new milking shed. With perseverance one would hardly expect from a cow used to barns and meadows, Polly walked half a mile up a track, navigated a crossroads, and avoided cars along a busy street — right back to where she lived before. Having charged ahead toward her goal, Polly was found, mooing at the gate.

Animals can also resolutely choose to stay with people they love, especially when those people have to go to a hospital. The devoted pet of a boy in West Virginia, a pigeon, banded unmistakably with the number 167, apparently became distressed when the boy was taken for surgery. The pigeon disappeared. But a week later, the boy heard fluttering at his hospital window. A nurse opened it, and in flew the pigeon, identified by his band. The bird had managed to fly seventy miles in a snowstorm, then found the right window in the dark. What incredible determination this must have involved.

Aggie, a husky mix in Ludington, Michigan, had been abused at some point in her life and was likely to cower at raised voices. But in her new home with guardian Barbara Olms, the dog's fear slowly diminished. She formed a fierce attachment to Olms and was apparently crestfallen when Olms had to go to the hospital. Aggie broke out of the yard and set out to find her.

"She definitely wanted to make sure I was okay. Evidently nothing could stop her," Olms says. Somehow, Aggie found the hospital, where she'd never been before. Then she broke inside,

Aggie reunited with Barbara Olms

and was thrown out, *three* times. At the third eviction, she tried so hard to stay at the hospital that the staff had to team up with police and an animal control officer to chase Aggie down and grab her.

Aggie was taken to the Mason County Animal Control facility and locked up in a small cage. I've seen photos of her behind bars, and in her eyes is undeniable despair. But there's also a glint of determination along with a little defiance, as if she's waiting for the chance to make her move and bolt again to find her guardian.

Aggie never lost sight of her goal, not even when Frances Sinnott, president of Lakeshore Animal Friends, rescued her and brought her home. "She didn't whine or cry, but she wasn't enthusiastic about anything. The spark had gone out of her," Sinnott remembers. In the house, Aggie moped and grieved with mournful eyes. During walks, she'd thrust her head forward and stare intently in only one direction.

One day when Sinnott opened her gate to put Aggie into the car, the dog shot off like a rocket—in exactly the direction she'd been focusing on. Aggie dashed down an alley, and, whimpering excitedly, she leapt into the arms of a young boy—who turned out to be Olms's grandson. Aggie, at last, had gotten to her guardian, now home from the hospital.

"Everyone thwarted Aggie's efforts, but in every instance she kept trying," Sinnott says. "Her heart was with Barbara. To get to her, Aggie was determined to overcome any obstacle that got in her way." Aggie's strength was apparent in her unbending will and her drive to stay her course. Part of that strength may well have been a virtue that Aggie already possessed. But another part surely was encouraged in her by Olms's love and kindness after the dog's early abuse.

According to veterinarian Michael Weiss, "If people treat animals with the same love they'd want for themselves, the animals have more heart and fight." In other words, our love may give animals strength. But the opposite is also true: When animals love and support us, *we* become stronger. There's a circle, a synergy. It's important and it's beautiful. Animals don't just choose to show strength in the seven ways I've described; they also choose to give strength to others.

When I adopted my cat, Linguine, she was sickly and frightened from past abuse. I nurtured her and gave her strength to overcome her difficult start in life. Several years later, I was lying on my bed in terrible pain from four injured discs in my spine. Every day for months, Linguine would jump on the bed, snuggle up to me, purr, and give me the strength to endure until I healed.

Linguine

Noble, my usually powerful, ferocious German shepherd, melts into a puddle of terror at the vet. To give Noble strength for exams and injections, I stand by him and hug him. In return, when I am nervous at being home alone at night, he stands by me and gives me the strength I need sometimes to peer out the window into the darkness to discover the source of a noise that has alarmed me.

Recently I met a woman who has multiple sclerosis and is always accompanied by her black Lab service dog, Murphy, a sturdy, robust animal, who seems proud to sport his red harness and backpack. This woman is often so weak that she can't hold up her head, so she props it, tilted at an angle, against her wheelchair's headrest. Though she has so little strength, Murphy offers her the courage to go out into the world. His presence, she says, sustains her, braces her physically and emotionally, and makes her feel strong.

At the same time, she makes Murphy strong. She rescued him from a shelter and taught him to be a service dog. This job has given him a purpose, and, as a result, he almost seems to embody force and determination. I've seen the woman grab his harness, and he pulls her along with such an intense focus that even teasing cats or freshly sautéed hamburger could not distract him from his mission. Once when I took hold of his leash to lead him to an elevator, he dug his paws into the carpeting and refused to budge. He didn't want to be taken so many steps away from his partner, I realized, so he was pitting all his muscles against my tug.

Murphy's guardian has made him maybe twice the dog he would have been without her. Because of their relationship, he's a mountain of fortitude and character. And so is she. This circle of strength between animals and people is a powerful force. It's an undeniable force for the good.

6.

COOPERATION

As we've learned in chapter 2, many living things are capable of exhibiting compassion. I was surprised to discover that even primeval cellular green slime mold does, too. A single-celled, amoeba-like creature, it slithers along damp forest litter and eats nutrients in its path. When food runs low, the mold sends out desperate chemical signals to other nearby slime mold cells, and a few million of them gather together to form a multi-celled organism called a grex. With no brain or central command, the grex somehow moves along like an inchworm and climbs out of the shadows of the forest to the light. The individuals in the forward part of the grex then die and form a stalk, so the ones in the rear can climb up it and get released into the environment to start a new search for food.

Psychologist Ross Buck theorizes that those forward green-slime cells who sacrifice themselves and die for others exhibit empathy—and even a fundamental, microscopic version of compassion. I think the grex is more strongly showing cooperation, another virtue that animals choose to exhibit. Just like the forward and the rear grex cells, animals often team up, depend on each other, and work toward a common goal. Animals come to each other's aid and get a job done together. They cooperate with a can-do attitude that's worthy of our notice.

Until recently, however, most scientists ignored animal cooperation and focused mostly on Charles Darwin's natural selection and survival of the fittest. They saw animals as ruthlessly competitive, locked in a fierce struggle for existence in a world where aggression ruled and the strong picked off the weak. Scientists took this view because cooperation seemed to make no sense in terms of evolution. It was assumed that "cheaters" would always take advantage of cooperative animals without giving anything back, so cheaters would be more likely than cooperators to survive and reproduce. The good guys, who tried to get along and help each other, were more likely to die out.

Because most scientists held on to this belief during their research into human and animal behavior, they weren't expecting to come across much animal cooperation in nature. And as biologist David Sloan Wilson says, "If you don't expect something, you never see it. One has to go out and look for it to find it."

Fortunately, Wilson and a small minority of scientists *have* gone out and looked, and they've found that, in the words of Lee Dugatkin, a biologist at the University of Louisville, "cooperation exists all around. I'd venture to say that in virtually every species living in a social group, you'd find cooperation going on in one way or another." Furthermore, these scientists have discovered that animal groups who cooperate actually do better than groups who don't. Contrary to the assumptions of some of their colleagues, these scientists have concluded that working together can enhance survival and well-being. Cooperation makes evolutionary sense after all, it seems.

Lee Dugatkin lists three basic ingredients for cooperation:

First and most important, it requires some kind of coordinated effort. Some species of ants on the move, for instance, coordinate themselves like insect Roman soldiers. When they're all trying to get from one tree to another, they will build a bridge with their bodies, so others can climb across. If some ant species are going to a termite nest on a hunting expedition, they'll coordinate by lining up two to ten abreast and marching in columns, which can vary from three to more than fifty feet in length. Ants also work as a team to transport prey back home. By sharing the burden, they can carry more weight and prevent ruffian ants from coming along and pirating their booty.

Honeybees coordinate in many ways, too, but I especially like their sharing chores in teams at home. Whatever tasks need to be done in the hive, they seem to take on cooperatively, even if a job is not their usual one. When their honeycomb needs repairing or remodeling, for instance, construction worker bees can call on bee guards or foragers to come and help. In hot weather, those foragers might bring home water, instead of the usual food. Then all the workers will pitch in and spread a thin liquid layer over the larval cells to cool them. When bees coordinate, their hive is like an insect commune, with one for all and all for one.

Coordination is essential for all species' reproduction. When you think about it, without cooperating, mating wouldn't meet with much success. Perhaps the maters who coordinate in the most unusual manner are small aquatic worms of the species *Ophryocha diadema*. Though they're simultaneous hermaphrodites, meaning that they have both male and female reproductive organs at once, they are never so sullenly antisocial as to mate with themselves. Instead, they find a cooperative partner.

Interestingly, as they mate from a few to dozens of times, they take turns donating sperm and egg. The reason for alternating is said to be because giving sperm is easy, but eggs require more energy and food resources to produce. If one of the worms insists on providing sperm only, the other one stops the tryst and leaves. Reversing roles to reproduce requires a give-and-take coordination.

Dugatkin's second ingredient for cooperation is cost. Individuals have to extend themselves, put out effort, and sacrifice in order for their behavior to be called cooperative. The cost can be in terms of providing energy and hard work, or giving up something that the animal itself would like to have, or facing danger and risking injury or death.

In one of the oddest examples of animal cooperation I've ever found, so called "cleaner fish" and their predators seem to pay all these prices at once. These fish maintain stations—which I picture in my mind as small, underwater beauty salons—around ocean shipwrecks or coral colonies. Like unkempt clients, predator fish will line up and wait their turn to be groomed by the cleaner fish. There are at least fifty species of cleaner fish, who swim forth and eat parasites and other potentially health-threatening foreign matter off the predators. The cleaners are so thorough that they even swim into the predators' mouths and nibble food particles between their teeth. The predators will patiently open their mouths for this dental attention, and they also obligingly move their gills to let the cleaners get into crevices for a more thorough job.

The cleaners' cost for this operation is work and energy and exposing themselves to danger; a predator could always succumb to the temptation to cheat and snap up the cleaner fish for a snack. At the same time, the predators' cost is controlling themselves and not gobbling down the snack that they undoubtedly would like to eat. If the predators happen to come across the cleaner fish at another location, in fact, they won't hesitate for an instant to devour them. Away from the station, this cooperative arrangement goes out with the tide.

When the predator and cleaner fish *are* at the station, though, it's all business, and they go to so much effort to work together in order to get, respectively, grooming and a meal. They're after the third ingredient that Dugatkin says is necessary to call an act cooperative: There's a reward, a positive outcome from putting out the effort. "Individuals get more in life by cooperating than by not cooperating," he explains. "They do better than if they hadn't worked together." As they team up, a payoff, supposedly, is their motivation.

But I don't find payoffs to be consistently apparent in demonstrations of animal cooperation, any more than I saw it in examples of compassionate or loyal animal behavior. Sure, when animals team up to work with others, sometimes they're looking for a reward or trying to promote their own well-being. But sometimes they're not. It depends on the circumstances. And in all the stories I've collected, I can tell you that circumstances vary greatly.

For example, Khayhim, an African hawk eagle, was stolen as a fledgling from his nest, then passed around for years to abusive people. He was extremely hostile about this treatment; even after he was brought to Lorna Stanton's rehabilitation center, he remained extremely dangerous and aggressive. Stanton tried to help Khayhim recover psychologically by taking him to fly, free, at a nearby nature reserve.

On one late afternoon outing, the eagle caught one of his wings on thorns as he soared down and landed in a thorn tree. The more desperately he thrashed to free himself, the more he got entangled, and soon both his wings were hooked. Stanton drove her microbus under the tree, stood on its roof, and tried to free him but couldn't quite reach. She knew that at dusk, other birds of prey would show up and possibly kill Khayhim for dinner. So Stanton had to hurry and find a way to get him down.

After trying unsuccessfully to climb the tree, Stanton finally attached a steel cable to the trunk of her vehicle, and, with a motorized winch, she pulled the top branches down toward the ground. Khayhim, who was normally so hostile and aggressive, stayed absolutely still while the tree bent down. He offered no resistance as Stanton freed his wings from the thorns. "He never bit or clawed me, even though his feet and beak were free," Stanton says. "It's almost like he was thinking, 'If I don't pull myself together and cooperate, she can't rescue me.'" Clearly, Khayhim's reward for cooperation was his own freedom.

More debatable is whether personal gain motivated three horses to cooperate with each other to save Skeeter, a colt. The baby animal was the first thing Doll Stanley worried about when she heard coyotes howl one night around Project Hope, the animal sanctuary she runs in Grenada, Mississippi. Not long before, a coyote had gone after goats and pigs in her barn, and she was afraid that it was coming back for the vulnerable and defenseless colt. She ran outside, armed with only a flashlight, and was ready to scream at the top of her lungs to scare off any predators.

But she needn't have bothered. When she arrived at the barn, she saw that Skeeter's mother, father, and sister had formed a protective circle around him. They were standing, nose to tail, in a ring so tight that all Stanley could see of Skeeter was his spindly little legs below the horses' bellies. His family was working as a team to keep him safe.

Many scientists would say that the horses were out to benefit themselves by kin selection and were driven to preserve their genes. But I disagree. I think that the horses were cooperating out of affection and concern. Caring, not selfishness, lay behind their teamwork. Their reward for cooperating was to have Skeeter, alive.

A similar goal must also have prompted the teamwork of

three collies, named Aireachail, Valkyrie, and Lyanan by their guardian, Mary Lou Wells, to match their Scottish heritage. Like a trio of Lassies, they would lie around the yard on Wells's farm in Kingston, Tennessee, and often seemed to watch protectively after her three-year-old daughter, Keira.

One day when Wells was washing the lunch dishes, the dogs suddenly barked a loud, fast, something-is-wrong bark. Wells hurried to the living room to check on Keira, and found that the child had disappeared. This wasn't necessarily an emergency, since her daughter occasionally wandered outside alone. But when the collies kept barking so urgently, dread crept into Wells's mind.

She rushed to the front door and looked up the hill at her horse paddock. She saw one horse, who'd been boarding with her, jump back from Wells's own three horses as if it had just bitten or kicked them. Wells could tell that something was wrong when all four of the animals whirled around and galloped, frightened, through the paddock gate, which was usually chained and locked but had somehow gotten open. Wells saw that Keira was standing out in the yard—directly in the path of eight pairs of thundering hooves.

From the front door, Wells yelled at the horses to stop. But the frightened horse in the lead kept going, straight toward Keira, then jumped over her at the last minute. A hoof hit Keira in the head and knocked her down.

"Whoa! Whoa!" Wells shouted. She ran outside, desperate to reach Keira before the other three horses got to the yard and pounded her into the ground. Though the collies were barking, they would be no help, Wells assumed, because the horses had stepped on them before. Pain had taught the dogs to hang back, shy of hooves. All the collies would do was add to the confusion.

Wells was wrong. Barking and growling and snarling, the

collies planted themselves between Keira and the horses. In some mysterious way, they communicated with each other and coordinated to protect the little girl. Each dog picked one horse, charged, lunged at it, and stopped it. Then working as a herding team, the collies moved the horses back away from the yard. Finally, while two of the dogs held the horses safely at a distance, the third ran to Keira and licked the tears off her cheeks.

In this incident, the collies had nothing to gain by working together. In fact, from past bad experiences with the horses, they knew there might be a painful cost for their teamwork. Yet they joined together, risked getting hurt, and coordinated for the benefit of Keira's safety, not their own gain. Freely choosing to cooperate, the collies took the moral high road.

Researchers have told me that the tendency to cooperate is probably innately programmed in the genes of simple organisms, such as the green slime mold. But more cognitively complex animals, like the collies, probably learn to cooperate as they grow up. The predisposition to *learn* to work with others is thought to be genetic, so genes, in other words, direct these animals toward the lessons of cooperation.

But animals are free to decide whether or not they'll be team players; and, as you might expect, some animals choose to work with others and some don't. Explains biologist David Sloan Wilson, "When it comes to cooperation, animals can be as varied as we can."

Two chimps, Becky and Jackie, show clearly this variety in cooperation. For decades, they were kept at a resort hotel in Cameroon and were cruelly isolated in separate, dismal, seven-foot-square cages. Veterinarian Sheri Speede, who was building an animal rehabilitation sanctuary nearby, arranged to adopt the chimps and went to see them regularly while getting ready to transport them to her facility. On each visit Becky would reach through the cage and hold Speede's hand. "For the first couple of times, she was really sweet," Speede says.

All that changed at the end of one afternoon's visit when Speede gathered up her belongings and told Becky that she had to go. Becky read the signals and understood that she was about to be left alone again. Desperate for company, she grabbed the hem of Speede's dress and tugged it inside the cage. Speede tugged back to keep her bottom from being exposed, but she knew that if she yanked too hard, the buttons down her dress front might pop open, and she'd be left standing there, blushing, in her underwear.

Speede pleaded with Becky to let her go. "But she wasn't having any of it," Speede says. "She pulled my dress as if to say, 'No, you're *not* going.'" Then, to emphasize her point, Becky, with her free hand, poured all the water from her bottle on the cage floor and used Speede's dress as a towel to wipe up the puddle.

Speede scolded, cajoled, reasoned, begged, and tugged for one of the longest half-hours of her life. But Becky, refusing to cooperate, kept her iron grip on Speede's dress until the hotel owner happened by and Speede shouted for help. The owner brought Speede a few apples, which she used to barter with Becky for her freedom.

Becky's companion, Jackie, had been so damaged psychologically by the years of misery and isolation he'd endured at the hotel that he would grab people who came near his enclosure at Speede's sanctuary, pull them toward him, and bite them. Slowly, though, he seemed to realize that Speede had brought him to a far better life than he'd had before. Making a huge turnaround, he began to hug and kiss the other chimps often, as well as Speede.

His behavior changed from uncooperative hooligan to cooperative primate Eagle Scout. The other chimps would toss their milk cups to the floor for Speede to pick up every day, but Jackie always politely handed his cup to her. One day without her ever asking at all, he went around the enclosure and gathered up *all* the chimps' cups. Then he gave the cups to Speede, in a gesture of willingness to work together.

When animals coordinate with each other or with us, they can forget their own needs and give freely. If they have jobs to do, they sometimes work so hard that their industry and effort are exemplary. In these respects, animals have lots to teach us about teamwork.

I've collected hundreds of examples of animals demonstrating cooperation in the workforce. In my files are stories of Italian housecats who worked together to perform as a troupe, swinging from trapezes, balancing on high wires, and lying on their backs to juggle with their feet. At the behest of his human "boss," one ferret threaded wires through forty-foot conduits in order to connect two military supercomputers. I've read of a canary who acted as assistant to a magician, and a search-and-rescue horse who drags other horses out of quicksand. There are dolphins in Florida who tow children with cancer around a lagoon to raise their morale as they fight their illness.

Lots of different kinds of animals cooperate with us at work, but by far the most common employees are dogs. When given tasks to do, most dogs are extremely responsible, committed workers. In important ways, they show cooperation at its very best.

First, dogs can cooperate by being willing to do whatever we ask. And, let me tell you, they have taken on unusual jobs. One day Charlie, a golden retriever, trotted out to a car at his guardian, Rick Parsons's, gas station in Saline, Michigan. The customer, on a whim, put a dollar bill for the gas in the dog's mouth. Charlie brought the money to Parsons, who traded a dog biscuit for it. From that point on, Charlie apparently believed he had a job to do. Every day for years, he would bring cash and credit cards to Parsons. Eager to cooperate, he saved Parsons miles of walking between gas pumps and cash register.

Molly, a yellow Lab from Leeds, Alabama, cooperates with her human guardian through her job as "balldog." She has learned to distinguish a foul ball from a fair ball by the sound it makes when hit with the bat. "She quickly figured out that 'this is my job,' " says her guardian, Jim Parramore. "At my son's ballpark, she's all business."

Out of thousands of hits at that park and at others, Molly had a hundred percent recovery rate and was credited one year with saving $850 in lost balls. A player once hit a ball outside the park into a river, and Molly dived down six feet to retrieve it. At another game she brought back a ball that had landed in a nearby pine plantation. The game ball had been lying in the middle of at least thirty others, but Molly found it in seconds—possibly by its new-leather smell. Major league scouts have asked Parramore if they could rent her to retrieve balls at baseball camps.

Magna, a mahogany-and-white stray of unknown lineage, also eagerly took on a highly unusual job. She was abandoned in a grocery store parking lot until Father Roy Swipes brought her to his

Magna and Father Roy Swipes

rectory at Our Lady of Guadalupe Church in Mission, Texas. "She seemed to know immediately that the church was where she was going to be," he says. "The people were Magna's flock. She was going to take care of them, like a shepherd." Almost immediately, he and Magna began to cooperate as a pastoral team in what he describes as "the most beautiful partnership."

Wearing church "robes" made for her by members of the congregation, Magna would walk down the aisle with Father Roy for five masses every Sunday. She would stand beside him during homilies, accompany him to greet parishioners with the sign of peace, and sit beside him when he handed out the host. Magna participated in weddings, baptisms, and first communions, and, afterward, if people were taking photographs, she'd continue cooperating on the job by walking over and getting in the picture. "She'd pose forever because she assumed that's what people wanted," explains Father Roy. During confessions and pastoral counseling sessions, she would lay her head in the laps of distressed parishioners to console them.

To assist Father Roy, she would also protect their flock by growling at unruly parishioners. And once when the parish teenagers put on a play about their patron saint, Maria Goretti—and a boy pulled a knife out of his tunic to "stab" her in front of the altar—Magna growled and leapt to her feet. Her hackles up, she jumped through the air, grabbed the teenager's wrist in her teeth, and shook the knife out of his hand. She'd thought that she'd been watching a real-life attack, and not a play. To her, cooperating as a churchdog meant keeping people safe.

Giving their hearts to a job is another way in which dogs can show cooperation at its best. Because they often seem genuinely concerned about performing their duties, they bring impressive dedication and commitment to their teamwork.

Exemplary in this respect are disaster dogs. After earthquakes, fires, floods, and bomb blasts, these animals work in teams with their handlers to look for survivors and to recover bodies. The dogs are well aware of the devastation around them. Says New Hampshire search-and-rescue dog handler Annabella Morse, whenever her German shepherd found a drowned victim, he made "a horrifying sound, like a cry. It was as though he recognized the death."

These dogs' dedication to their job became obvious after the Alfred P. Murrah federal building in Oklahoma City was bombed and disaster dogs arrived on a scene grisly beyond description. Along with the death they surely sensed, they had to contend with glass shards and sharp pieces of steel that cut their paws. Extremely eager to cooperate, the dogs started out attentive, their eyes bright, their tails wagging. When the dogs smelled or heard a person buried in the rubble, they would alert their handlers by barking, sitting, whining, or digging.

But once no more people were being found alive, the dogs flattened back their ears, drooped their tails, and became depressed and subdued. One handler said her Lab-husky mix wanted to sit in her lap for reassurance. Others reported that their dogs refused to eat or play while taking breaks. To boost their dogs' spirits, the handlers sometimes got team members to hide under the debris so that the dogs could "rescue" them. In spite of their despair, the dogs kept cooperating and searching.

While, to me, this shows just how committed these animals were to their work, some of the handlers feel otherwise. According to Sergeant Lyndell Easley of the Oklahoma City Police Canine Unit, the dogs became glum because they weren't getting praise, petting, or tennis ball tosses as payoffs for locating live people. "The dogs just respond to their training," he told me. "If they're conducting a search and aren't successful, then they don't get a reward. So their motivation goes away."

Other handlers told me that the dogs became subdued only because they picked up stress and negative emotions in their handlers' voice, body language, and facial expressions. "The dogs were so tuned into their handlers that they were reading that something was wrong and the handler was upset," says Stephen Croteau, a Rhode Island dog handler. "The psychological depression of the handlers extended down the leash."

But William Thomason, a Canyon Lake, Texas fireman on the scene, interpreted the dogs' behavior as I do. He noted that once a dog located a survivor, it was often impossible to drag the animal away until the person was given medical attention. The dogs were as concerned about the injured people as the rescuers were, Thomason believed. Giving their big hearts to their work made their cooperation especially impressive.

Dogs can also show cooperation at its best by eagerly putting not just their feelings, but also their unique talents into their work. To get a job done, they can be generous with those talents, which may be tied to the dogs' individual temperament. Some dogs demonstrate cooperation by using their innate gentleness and sensitivity, or physical speed, strength, or sharpness of vision or hearing. Dogs often seem never to tire of making their gifts available and giving all they have to cooperative ventures.

Umbra, a Lab mix in Illinois, for instance, brings her natural gift for swimming to her work as a hearing dog for her guardian, Ted Erikson. Erikson, a former record-holding marathon swimmer, can't hear approaching motor boats or jet skis while he does his workouts in the water of Lake Michigan, and so Umbra will swim alongside him every day, sometimes for miles. Zeus, a Great Pyrenees, donates his natural heft, patience, and alertness when he guards twenty-five-hundred sheep in Idaho; his I'll-take-care-of-you attitude is as reliable as the sunrise, apparently, as he zealously keeps his flock safe from bears and coyotes, day and night. Then there's Max, a golden retriever, who never fails to put his innate friendliness into his job as a therapy dog at Wittenberg University's Math Workshop in Springfield, Ohio. With radar-like perceptiveness, he identifies tense students and goes straight to every one of them to offer soothing as they pore over complicated formulas and theories.

Other cooperative dogs eagerly volunteer their exquisitely sensitive noses to locate truffles, drugs, and termites. When the Swedish parliament decreed that old industrial stocks of mercury had to be located and properly disposed of, two dogs worked so hard that in just two years they found more than ten *tons* of the hazardous substance, illegally hidden in drains, electrical equipment, and labs. AJ, a droopy, wrinkled bloodhound, offers his nose on searches for Pet Hunters, a Santa Cruz, California pet-detective agency. His partner, former police officer Kat Albrecht, sometimes uses high-tech infrared cameras, surveillance devices, and DNA tests in order to solve cases, but she relies mostly on AJ's unrelenting sniffing. As his nose skims the ground like a vacuum cleaner with no "off" switch, he's helped her track down lost cats, dogs, and horses, a turtle, a snake, and an iguana.

On a hunt last year for Bubba, a Jack Russell terrier who had escaped from his yard, Albrecht commanded AJ to "take scent," and he snapped to attention. He seemed almost to inhale Bubba's wool blanket; then, at the command, "search," AJ bounded off as if his whole life depended on discovering Bubba's traces. For blocks, AJ tugged Albrecht along sidewalks, over lawns, and across flowerbeds. They passed through one neighborhood, then another, until AJ yanked Albrecht down a tree-lined street toward a small white house. When a woman stopped her van and learned what they were looking for, she told them she'd found Bubba. He was in her garage—in the very house AJ had been heading toward.

Tess

Dogs' focus on the task at hand can be so sharp that they seem indifferent to anything else around them. For example, Karelian bear dogs, which have a husky's shape and body and a panda's black-mask eye markings, can be unrelenting in their focus on doing what they were put on earth to do. And that is cooperating with their handler to track bears — and to turn them, chase them, and tree them. Even when the dogs are asleep, they're ready to spring to their feet and become bear-controlling machines. One hint of a grizzly, and the dogs' urgently purposeful streak reigns supreme.

I've seen them bring this intense focus to their work with bear biologists Carrie Hunt and Tim Manley, who teach grizzlies to behave in a manner that doesn't put them in conflict with people. Using rubber bullets, cracker shells, and pepper spray, the team will convey to bears that they must stay away from houses and campgrounds. To underscore Hunt and Manley's lessons, the bear dogs contribute violent barks and unrelenting chases. Working together, Hunt, Manley, and the dogs have prevented dozens of marauding bears from having to be killed for the sake of people's safety.

One night, Hunt and Manley took two of the dogs, Cassie and Tess, to a Montana hunter's tent, where a grizzly had come looking for food and had refused to leave — even when the hunter had fired eight shots above the bear's head. Suddenly, the bear burst out of the trees near the tent. Cassie and Tess went crazy with barking while Manley shot rubber bullets and cracker shells at the bear, and he ran away.

Grizzlies, named *Ursus arctos horribilis*—the "horrible" bear because they are so fierce—can flip over boulders, rip trees apart, tear flesh with up to five-inch claws. They loom like monsters over a forty-to-sixty-pound bear dog. Still, all night long, as Hunt, Manley, and the hunter waited in the tent to teach the bear to stay away, the dogs never flinched as the bear sneaked back into the campsite repeatedly.

The grizzly had been trapped before and was wearing a radio collar, so Manley and Hunt were able to detect his distance and direction. But even before the high-tech equipment could locate him, Cassie and Tess were able to pick up his scent and quiet crunches in the underbrush. Every time he approached, they would point at him like compass needles. Whenever the bear came close, Hunt and Manley took the dogs outside to face him down. The dogs would lunge from the end of their leashes to attack, holding him back each time he circled around and came in from a new direction. Finally, just before dawn, the bear slipped away into the woods and disappeared. The dogs' determination had won out over his.

Other dogs have worked even longer and under worse conditions than Cassie and Tess. In 1929, residents of Nome, an Alaskan town that was icebound for seven months a year, needed vials of diphtheria serum in order to stop an epidemic that was about to sweep through town. Three children had already died, and every minute counted. But in those days airplanes' open cockpits prevented Alaska flights in winter, and the closest a train could carry the serum was to the town of Nenana, 674 miles away. So the governor of Alaska asked mushers and their sled-dog teams to run a relay from Nenana to Nome.

The drivers and dogs would transport the twenty-pound package of serum in the same way that they often transported water, food, mail, and hunting supplies. With a lead dog finding the trail and guiding the others, the team would pull together as fast as they could. Their lives—and the lives of the Nome residents—hinged on the dogs' endurance, strength, speed, courage, intelligence, and, most of all, cooperation with each other and their musher. Day and night, the dogs worked together in extremely perilous conditions.

On January 27, the first team set out. The temperature dropped from thirty to fifty degrees below zero. The next day, five more teams kept the serum moving as new snow fell and the wind picked up. If wind blows at sled dogs from the side, it drives "spindrift," a shower of fine snow, into the dogs' undercoat and destroys its insulation. That leaves the dogs vulnerable to hypothermia and frostbite. The dogs' eyes also can ice up; snow accumulates around the rims and must be frequently removed.

On the relay's third day, as weather conditions turned from perilous to nightmarish, two dogs froze right on their feet. To the moment of their deaths, the dogs had been trying to cooperate. On the fourth day, a team led by the famous sled dog Togo took a shortcut across the frozen Norton Sound as hurricane-force winds threw stinging seawater into their eyes. The jagged, cracking ice floes the team crossed over broke up just a few hours afterward.

Blinding, disorienting snow enveloped the next team, and a roaring blizzard, the next. The last team, led by the half-wolf, half-malamute Balto, forged ahead even though no one believed that any musher and dogs would possibly brave—let alone survive—the storm, no matter how willing they were to work together in the terrible conditions. Though another team was supposed to relieve that team twenty-one miles from Nome, the waiting driver had fallen asleep and was not ready to travel his leg of the relay. So Balto and his sledmates kept going as eighty-mile-an-hour winds twice blew them straight up into the air.

Finally, Balto led his teammates down a street to the door of Nome's hospital, where they collapsed. Sharp pieces of ice were stuck in the dogs' bleeding, freezing paws. But Nome's people had their serum. Altogether, the twenty teams in the relay made the trip in a little less than five and a half days. The sled dogs in each relay team had cooperated with each other and their musher to work and survive in a frozen hell.

Other amazingly cooperative dogs have done the same in a different kind of hell: the hell of war. I've seen films of dogs being parachuted into European battle zones and shot at while carrying messages and guarding wounded soldiers. In the Vietnam War, approximately four thousand Labrador retrievers and German shepherds were sent to guard U.S. military facilities; track down the enemy; find their mines, booby traps, and supply caches; and search their tunnels, where poisonous snakes, tied by the tail from the ceiling, were waiting for them. The dogs who cooperated in perhaps the harshest conditions were the scout dogs, who "walked point," meaning that, in the most vulnerable, forward position, they led patrols to locate, observe, and destroy the enemy. By cocking their heads, twitching their muscles, pricking their ears, or giving other subtle, silent signals, the dogs alerted their handlers to danger before the platoon could be ambushed.

"The Vietnam War was a guerrilla war, an ambush war. You were fighting someone you couldn't see," explains Jessie Mendez, a scout dog trainer who served three tours of duty. At any moment snipers or hidden enemy forces could blast the dogs, with their handlers, out of existence. (The North Vietnamese gave rewards for pairs of German shepherd ears as proof of death.) The dogs also faced mines, snares, tripwires attached to bombs, and pungi stakes of sharpened bamboo, dipped in human feces in order to cause quick infections. Stepping on a vine could bring a big, spiked ball swinging down from the trees. Falling into a camouflaged pit could mean landing on snakes or upturned spikes.

The dogs, often exhausted from double or triple duty and Vietnam's debilitating, muggy heat, kept cooperating. One animal, Ringo, was badly wounded and left behind in an emergency evacuation. But he managed to survive in the jungle for days until he made his way back to base. There, even while he was bleeding, starving, and dehydrated, he indicated that he was eager to resume his scout-dog work.

Polar Bear, another German shepherd, was wounded in his face and shoulder while on a mission to flush out North Vietnamese soldiers from a bunker complex. Taken back to Tay Ninh base, the dog was so traumatized from his wounds that he wouldn't let anyone near him. He was chained to a stake and given a new job as sentry at a command bunker, where Paul Morgan, a Green Beret fire support coordinator, came upon him, starving and frantically pacing back and forth.

Morgan gave Polar Bear bread, fish, and water, and held him while a medic cleaned his wounds. Upon learning that the dog was going to be put down as "salvage equipment," Morgan sneaked him into his own bunker at Fire Base Diana, near Cambodia. Removed from the official scout-dog role, Polar Bear was no longer expected to cooperate with anyone, and he could lie around, permanently off duty.

But one night a regiment of fifteen hundred North Vietnamese soldiers broke through the razor wire surrounding the base and attacked three hundred U.S. soldiers. While mortars exploded in terrifying flashes and shrapnel screamed through the air, Morgan hid behind a bunker to direct helicopter gunships by radio. "Because Polar Bear had been wounded, he'd lost his nerve," Morgan says. The dog leaned, shaking, against his knee.

Then suddenly, Polar Bear, barking fiercely, ran to a trench just a few feet from Morgan. Assuming that the dog was alerting them to danger, a fellow soldier followed Polar Bear and opened fire in the trench. Morgan later saw that two enemy soldiers, who'd been about to attack, were lying in the trench, dead. Though Polar Bear had so recently been wounded, and though he'd never trained to work with Morgan, "he came right back to being a scout dog. He started operating again," Morgan says.

Later, Morgan was badly wounded. After he was evacuated, he heard from his colleagues that the dog still patrolled the base and continuously watched and listened for the North Vietnamese. He chose to resume his work. "The scout dogs were so totally dedicated," Morgan says. "They were perfect about cooperating."

You might expect carefully trained military dogs to cooperate because duty is strictly required of them. But often equally eager to do their jobs are service dogs, who often cooperate in quiet ways but can be heroic when they go beyond the call of duty.

Ike is an ordinary yellow Lab with an extraordinary work ethic. Says his partner, Elizabeth Twohy, director of disability services at Brookdale Community College in Lincroft, New Jersey, "Ike wants very much to please me, so he anticipates what I want. He's watching all the time to see if there are things he can do to help me."

Ike does such usual service-dog duties as pulling Twohy's wheelchair, carrying things for her, and bringing her the telephone. But he also sorts Twohy's recyclables into separate containers for garbage, cans, and bottles, and he very carefully gets dishes for her from the dishwasher. When Twohy tells him to "pack," Ike will pick up his dish, toys, and favorite bone—"the things he thinks are important," Twohy says—and set them in a bag for her.

Most amazing, Ike will wipe his paws, one at a time, on Twohy's doormat. She taught him to do this by first saying, "wipe paws," and praising him every time he moved his foot. Then she touched another foot, and then another, until he moved—and soon wiped—each one. Eventually, Towhy didn't even have to ask. Every time Ike comes inside, he tries so hard to cooperate that he wipes all four paws all by himself.

Another ultra-cooperative service dog is Shantih. As the dog was pulling the wheelchair of her partner, Jean King, up a ramp in a Pennsylvania snowstorm, the chair hit a patch of ice and slid backward. To stop King from rolling off the ramp, Shantih threw herself at the chair, lodged her body against it, and strained and pushed to keep King safe until help came. Shantih did this despite almost unbearable pain: As she held the chair, a ligament in her hind leg was slowly tearing.

In Washington state, Anna, a service hearing dog, who is a mix of Labrador retriever and Australian cattle dog, once jumped up on her partner, Barbara Biggs, when Biggs was on a horseback ride. Anna was trying to let Biggs know that a rattlesnake was coiled, ready to strike, in her path. In Sacramento, California, Mitzi, part golden retriever and part heaven-only-knows-what, grabbed the shirtsleeve of a mugger, who attacked her deaf partner, James Reeves. As a snarling protector and not just a hearing dog, Mitzi snapped and lunged and ran off the criminal. Cooperating on her job, she, too, went beyond the call of duty.

So did Kim, a black-and-tan mutt, who looks like a tiny German shepherd. She seemed to sense the chronic back pain of deaf university student, Randy Moering. Without being asked, she always treated him with special gentleness, and so he was stunned when, on a walk after a heavy windstorm in Washington, D.C., Kim yanked so hard on the leash that she pulled him off balance. Just as he stumbled backward, a huge tree limb crashed where he'd been walking. High in the tree was a storm debris cleanup crew, cutting limbs with a chainsaw that Moering could not hear.

Nigel, an extremely cooperative black Lab seeing-eye dog, also went an extra mile on his job. As he led Charles Nwosu along a street in Fayetteville, North Carolina, they heard a car motor running near an apartment building's driveway. Nigel stopped, and they waited for five minutes for the car to pass. When it didn't, Nwosu finally told Nigel, "forward." The dog obeyed.

In the middle of the driveway, Nigel suddenly leapt up on Nwosu and shoved him backward. Not understanding why the dog was being so rough, Nwosu resisted, so Nigel tried to tug him out of the driveway. As they struggled, Nwosu heard a terrible thud. The car hit the dog and pushed him against Nwosu with such force that they both flew through the air and fell in the street. As a woman in the car screamed, "Stop! You've killed them!" the driver revved his engine. With a squeal of tires, he sped away—and ran over the dog's foot.

Nigel had placed himself between Nwosu and the car in order to take the impact of the hit. Unconscious and badly injured, he was paying dearly for trying so hard to cooperate and do his job. Nwosu was sure that Nigel was dead, but when he touched the dog, Nigel vaguely moved his tail, a semi-conscious wagging with affection, Nwosu believed. After five or six minutes, Nigel regained full consciousness, and the first thing he did was lick Nwosu's face to comfort him.

"Can we make it home, Nigel?" Nwosu asked.

The dog struggled to his feet. When Nwosu took Nigel's harness, he could feel that the dog was trembling in pain. As Nigel limped along, he sometimes had to lie down on the sidewalk to rest. But each time he forced himself up again until he finally brought Nwosu to his front door. Inside, Nigel lay at Nwosu's feet, still ready to serve. Nwosu's wife rushed the dog to a veterinarian, who said that Nigel had heroically shepherded his guardian half a mile to safety—walking on a broken leg.

When a vandal threw a brick at the car of Randy Moering, the missile injured Kim, his hearing dog. Devastated by her needless suffering, Moering later concluded that animals are like flowers popping up in the cracks of a sidewalk. Partly, he meant that against the vandal's hardness, anger, and cruelty was Kim's goodness, as beautiful as a flower. In a larger sense, Moering was also implying that in the "cracks" between the world's harshness and indifference are animals' love and eagerness to please.

When animals work so diligently to coordinate in teams with us, they can show that love and eagerness more than ever. They push ahead, indomitably, even in circumstances as difficult and inhospitable as cracks between slabs of concrete. So often willing to do whatever it takes to carry out a job, animals have much to teach us about cooperation—and about putting out effort and trying so hard.

7.

RESOURCEFULNESS

Last year I visited my favorite duck pond only to see it
drained dry. Normally, there's a big flock of birds paddling
around a fountain in the pond's center, showing off their gor-
geous feathers, and quacking and swimming in zigzags over to
people like me who bring them bread. Those napping on the
shore, heads tucked against their shoulders, will usually raise a
cautious eyelid to keep track of potentially dangerous people
and dogs.

When I arrived that afternoon, though, the place was dead.
According to a printed sign, no water would be pumped back
into the pond for three weeks. The ducks, in other words, had
lost their free food and safe haven. As I glanced around the desolate, empty pond, I felt desolate and empty, too. I worried about
those ducks.

They were so unprotected, compared to people, I thought. We
pick up our food at grocery stores; for water, we turn on faucets.
We've got laws and police to keep us safe and doctors and hospi-
tals to keep us healthy. And if we run out of money, we can generally turn to charities or welfare. In contrast, when a duck loses

its pond and free breadcrumbs, all that stands between life and death is its wits and a layer of feathers.

Life can be so hard for animals. It's a dog-eat-dog world out there. And when the going gets tough, they have to get going. If wild animals aren't careful every second of their lives, they can freeze, starve, die of thirst, or become a meal. And domestic animals don't always have it any easier. So often they end up lost, abandoned, or alone for some other reason—and they have to find food and shelter, fight off attackers, or get themselves out of trouble. On their own in a crisis, they have to figure out how to survive.

Given the insecurity, vulnerability, and hardship to which the animals are so often exposed, they can show remarkable strength and fortitude. Sometimes even more remarkable, though, is the resourcefulness they demonstrate. I've collected hundreds of examples of animals who draw upon their brains and natural talents to meet challenges cleverly and admirably. Animals often manage to develop the specific skills they need to get by in life, and they apply them when necessary. Or they take advantage of objects, and sometimes even people, that they find around them as a means for their survival and well-being. By resourcefully combining their own innate gifts with the material gifts available in their world, animals can seem enterprising, ingenious, and unbeatable.

Sometimes I find their resourcefulness not just amazing, but thrilling. Take, for example, the humble yellow pine chipmunk, an innocent, cuddly little creature if there ever was one. But it's also a dynamo of resourcefulness. Every year a chipmunk will preserve at least ten thousand nuts and seeds by burying them in different sites in its territory. To protect itself in case any of these sites are disturbed or their contents are stolen, the chipmunk leaves only one or two nuts and seeds in each place—so it has *seven to nine thousand* different caches of food. And the food itself is not the chipmunk's only resource. Even more important is the animal's memory. Studies by University of Nevada biologist Steven Vander Wall have shown that, astoundingly, the chipmunk doesn't find its thousands of stashes by smell, but by keeping in mind the location of nearby rocks, tree roots, logs, clumps of grass, and other landmarks.

Rather than gathering their food, other animals will hunt resourcefully for it. To do so, they use their physical weapons like strength, speed, teeth, and claws, of course, but they also draw on their mental ability to devise wily strategies. In South Africa, a pair of jackals was once seen lying in wait for a flock of vultures bathing in a river. The jackals delayed attacking the birds until their feathers were too heavy and sodden with water for them to make a quick escape. Then the jackals grabbed their dinner. A lion in South Africa, who was so old that her teeth were worn to nubs, would wait patiently at a waterhole until a hyena was distracted by drinking. Since the lion's dull teeth made her unable to kill prey in her usual way, by getting a stranglehold on an animal's neck or muzzle, she had learned to spring on her prey at the waterhole and kill it by drowning. This lion's teeth may have been gone, but her clever brain surely wasn't.

Animals can be incredibly resourceful not just to get food, but also to take care of their physical comfort. Elephants will grab sticks with their trunks to scratch themselves in hard-to-reach places. They use branches as flyswatters and clumps of grass as washcloths for their wounds. Chimpanzees will shelter their faces from the rain with hats and umbrellas they make out of leaves. They also use leaves for dinner napkins and toilet paper.

Chimps are also known to carefully gather, fold, and swallow small, new aspilla leaves, which they ingest, some researchers believe, because aspilla leaves contain thiarubrine-A, a potent compound that helps the chimps rid themselves of parasites.

I recently read about a beaver who must have disliked holding his breath while swimming under ice in winter. He cut a hole in his dam to lower the water level, a smart way to create space for oxygen below the ice ceiling. A young white rhino named Dips also solved a problem of discomfort after he got tired of shocks from the electric fence around his pen at South Africa's Wildcare. Before approaching the fence, Dips tipped the water out of his rubber trough and hung it on his horn. Dips repeatedly used this anti-shock armor until he got old enough to be released again into the wild.

All these instances of animal resourcefulness have proven to me that there was really no need to worry so much about those ducks who were turned out of their pond. Animals are extremely good at taking care of themselves. They are what we would call "street-smart." They're the ultimate survivors.

To my way of thinking, this kind of resourcefulness requires a level of thought, of reason, of problem solving. But some scientists suggest that animals' seemingly "smart" behavior is really a matter of instinct or conditioning. In other words, those experts say, animals will accidentally stumble upon an action that results in either a reward or a punishment; then the reward or punishment programs them to respond reflexively to whatever stimulus prompted that action. For example, just by chance a skunk may turn over a rock and discover insects underneath. So the skunk may then deliberately turn over more rocks in search of more insects. In the view of some, this is done mechanically, without thought or choice.

But I believe that it's impossible to see animals as machines because there are simply too many examples of deliberate animal resourcefulness and clever thinking. While animals often do behave according to instinct or conditioning, they are neither witless robots nor undeveloped humans with a duller version of our own minds. It's important not to see animals in either of these two extremes, but rather as being alert and thinking in their own animal way.

Alert thinking seems especially evident in the behavior of animals who are able to adapt and improvise when they find themselves in totally novel situations — such as, for example, when a pampered, well-provided-for household pet decides to take a solitary, long-distance journey. Sometimes a dog, cat, or bird will become separated from its human family by accident or when given away or abandoned. And a pet may find itself lost during a family trip or a household move. Whatever the cause of the animal's being on its own, it can end up striking out sometimes for incredible distances through unfamiliar territory to find its home again.

We can imagine the huge and constant obstacles that such an animal would have to overcome as it journeyed through ever-changing terrain and circumstances, made endless decisions about its direction of travel, and figured out how to obtain food and shelter. The animal would have to be extremely resourceful in order to survive.

Ninja, a fluffy, pampered, eight-year-old housecat, may have seemed an unlikely candidate for venturing forth into the unknown. But after his family moved from Farmington, Utah, to a Seattle suburb that he apparently didn't like, he set out on his own to return to his former residence. Somehow he found ways to cross 850 miles of rivers, mountains, and the countless perils found in Oregon's rugged Hood National Forest. One year and two months after setting out, the small cat finally sat down, thin and scraggly, but triumphant, on the second-story porch of his former home.

The family of Chat Beau, a half-Persian white cat, had left their home in Lafayette, Louisiana, in search of a new house in Texarkana, Texas, 294 miles away. Chat Beau had been left with a neighbor. The cat was distressed by his guardians' absence, however, and one day he simply disappeared. His family was forced to move permanently to Texarkana without knowing what had happened to him.

But one day four months after Chat Beau disappeared, he wandered up to the Texarkana school where the wife in his human family was a teacher and her son was a student. The family absolutely identified the cat by a scar over his eye, some tar that they'd never been able to get off his tail, and his habit of answering to whistles and, when angry, growling like a dog. Though Chat Beau had never been to Texarkana in his life and had followed no sensory trail to his family, he'd somehow managed to find them.

In France, a five-year-old spitz named Beethoven was separated from his family while on vacation near Avignon. The dog then started home to Nomeny—four hundred miles away. As he slogged along, he not only had to contend with terribly worn-down paw pads but also had to dodge cars on freeways, make his way safely through towns and wilderness areas, and find food and shelter during the lowest temperatures ever recorded in France in December and January. Somehow, he found the means to get home after nine months of travel, all the way from near the Mediterranean to the French/German border.

Snaggletooth, an eight-foot, 150-pound alligator, was easily identified by the crooked tooth from which she got her name. She was accustomed to living in a serene pond near the driving range of a South Miami golf course and was inconvenienced only by the occasional errantly-hit golf ball. She started snapping at club employees who came to retrieve the balls, however, and state biologists transferred her to Collier-Seminole State Park, 140 miles away.

Snaggletooth apparently decided that she wanted her secure and comfortable life in her pond again. So she swam all the way around the southern tip of Florida and encountered noisy boats, human predators, and unfamiliar terrain. Back on land, she traveled through all the dangers of human civilization and then walked to the golf course. Though her formerly easy life had probably not well prepared her for the difficulties she met on her trip, she somehow found the resources to handle them, nevertheless.

Emily, a huge but gentle black-and-white, fourteen-hundred-pound Holstein cow, was also incredibly resourceful in novel circumstances. She was standing on a loading dock in Sherborn, Massachusetts, next in line for the killing floor. When workers took a half-hour lunch break, the reprieve gave her enough time to figure out what was about to happen to her. She gathered

Emily

her wits, leapt over a five-foot stockade gate, and fled into the woods.

The slaughtermen searched for her for days. When they approached, she must have seen them from a hiding place and even at a distance smelled the blood on their white suits. Emily seemed to know exactly who these people were and why they wanted her. So she continued to elude them, and over the next few weeks one blizzard followed another in the snowiest New England winter in a decade. Though Emily was hungry, she refused to come near hay that the slaughtermen left as a lure.

A month after Emily's escape, a woman named Meg Randa heard that Emily had been sighted by many Sherborn residents as she wandered around town with icicles hanging from her whiskers. Randa, a vegetarian with deep convictions about animal rights, teaches special education classes and runs Vegan-peace, an animal sanctuary. She quickly arranged to purchase Emily from the slaughterhouse and then searched the woods for three days before finally discovering the cow's hiding place.

In an area sheltered by evergreen trees, Emily had cleared away the snow to find warmer, drier dirt in which to make herself a bed. Randa had seen the cow following a herd of deer, who presumably had shown her how to eat leaves and acorns and get fluids from snow. "That was an intelligent means of survival for a dairy cow who'd been fed and watered all her life," Randa says. It was amazingly resourceful behavior for a cow who'd never before had to run for her life in blizzards.

Like so many animals who find themselves in novel situations, Emily had relied on her own perceptiveness, good judgment, and creativity. She'd also used what resources presented themselves: the deer as teachers of survival skills, and the evergreens and acorns for shelter and sustenance. Even Randa and her safe home became resources for Emily when, after having lost five hundred pounds in five weeks, she allowed herself to be coaxed on a trailer and taken to Veganpeace.

Emily and all the journeying animals I've mentioned showed amazing resourcefulness for supporting themselves with food and shelter at the same time that they accomplished great feats of physical endurance or navigation. And the animals did all this in unfamiliar settings that required constant ingenuity and problem solving. But even animals who are in their normal territory can have their resourcefulness tested when they must protect themselves or obtain the food and shelter necessary for survival. Familiarity of surroundings does not necessarily lessen the challenge of earning a living.

To get along in life, these animals have to learn skills. And when they employ the skills, they have to make constant judgments and minute-to-minute choices about how to proceed. The animals have to be thinking as they work, just as we do. Their skills, in fact, often seem surprisingly similar to our own.

Some species of ants are farmers. These insects actually prepare fields and plant crops of fungus, which they prune to form the ball-shaped pieces they like to eat. Other kinds of ants are ranchers: They "herd" aphids to obtain a food called honeydew, which aphids excrete after feeding on plants with sugar-rich sap. The ants move a group of aphids along from plant to plant and even build little barns made of leaves to shelter them.

Birds, the Frank Lloyd Wrights of the animal world, apply construction skills. Tailorbirds, for example, sew fibers, like thread, through leaves to form a living cradle for their homes. Weaverbirds have conquered warp and weft for nest building. Ovenbirds will sculpt about two thousand beaksful of mud into domed nests that, with a coat of whitewash, could pass as very small adobe huts. These and other resourceful applications of knowledge and skill are what enable many animal species to meet their material needs.

In order to survive or get along with others, many animals put language skills to work. Prairie dogs, according to Con Slobodchikoff, a biologist at Northern Arizona University, possess "the most sophisticated natural language ever decoded in animals." Slobodchikoff has documented more than a hundred prairie dog words, including nouns for hawk, coyote, human, cat, and dog, and adjectives for colors, speeds, shapes, and sizes. The resourceful prairie dogs learn these words in order to keep themselves safe. They will emit one warning call to signal if a man, for instance, is approaching. They will modify the call to indicate the speed at which he is approaching and whether he's tall, short, carrying a gun, or wearing a blue or green shirt.

Regular domestic dogs can also use language skills as a resource. Juliette, a deaf dalmation from Spokane, Washington, learned American Sign Language in order to communicate with her human family. Chloe, a deaf Australian shepherd from Columbia, South Carolina, followed special hand signals that her guardian invented for her.

Though dogs are commonly taught to respond to hand signals, Juliette and Chloe had no prior experience with verbal commands or communication with humans. The dogs had somehow to grasp the concept that their guardians were visually "talking" to them, then figure out what the people were "saying." Both dogs were so resourceful that they quickly learned to sit, lie down, stay, and come when "asked" by hands. Juliette learned other words: "food," "hungry," and "out," for instance. And Chloe's guardian amazingly even taught her the word "no" by putting a stern look on her face and crossing her arms down sharply in an "x." The signals, though simple, let the dogs know what they needed to know in order to live in harmony with their human families.

To me, animals are most remarkably resourceful when they use dramatic skills to dupe others into believing what the animals want them to believe. Animals can be champion actors. In fact, many species of animals carry off theatrical performances that I'd say are worthy of Oscars.

Cichlid fish pretend to be lying around, dead as stones—until a smaller fish swims close. Then the cichlid springs to life and snaps it up. Zone-tailed hawks will rock their wings in flight, as vultures do, to trick their prey into a false sense of security (vultures normally do not attack live prey). When smaller birds grow inattentive, the hawks swoop down to kill.

In addition to hunting, some animals use acting skills to defend themselves. In desperate moments, hognose snakes can be downright melodramatic. When threatened, they mimic vipers and coil up, puffing themselves up, flattening their heads, then striking. If that drama isn't deterrence enough, the snakes will fake death in order to avoid what is perceived as an attack. They roll over, writhe, defecate, and go into contortions—and finally lie there, upside down, not visibly breathing, their tongues hanging out. Says Gordon Burghardt, a University of Tennessee ethologist, "They look like they've had a fit and died."

The snakes in Burghardt's lab studies *purposely* decided whether or not to pretend to be conked out. After a deceptive fit, they would tuck their tongues back in their mouths and slither off if the experimenter, whom they viewed as a threat, left the room. But if he continued to stand there, the snakes would keep up the dramatics. After repeated tests, the snakes even learned that the human wasn't going to hurt them, and they became blasé, and stopped bothering with viper and death acts.

Like hognose snakes, some primates draw on acting skills as a resource to defend themselves—only their drama is designed to wrench sympathy from bullies. In *Good Natured*, Frans de Waal, a zoologist and ethologist at Yerkes Regional Primate Research Center at Emory University, describes a captive male chimp who injured his leg in a fight. He developed a limp that lasted long after his leg was healed. The perfectly healthy chimp would hobble around, looking unthreatening and pitiful as a ruse to disarm the aggressive chimp that had previously beaten him up. At Wildcare, one old male chimpanzee, tired of constant harassment from dominant males, would grab the nearest baby chimp whenever the males came looking for a fight. Pretending to be engrossed in the infant, the resourceful old chimp was in fact using the baby as a shield, a deterrent from attacks.

Mongo, an enterprising Scottish terrier from Portland, Oregon, seemed to employ dramatic skills in pursuit of romance. After spending a few days at the clinic of his veterinarian, William Ruggles, he went home and spiraled into a major funk. Lying around and moping as if he were severely ill, Mongo limped on what appeared to be a badly injured paw. His guardian brought him back to the vet, and Mongo hobbled gingerly into the clinic. When placed on the steel examination table, he held up his front paw as if the pain were excruciating.

Ruggles proclaimed Mongo perfectly healthy and set him on the floor again. Without a moment's hesitation, the dog, suddenly limp-free and energetic, dashed to the area where he'd been caged just days before. He bounded up to a female dog, whom he had, apparently, badly wanted to see again. Mongo's feigned limp and illness, Ruggles believes, had been his dramatic ploy for getting back to the clinic for a tryst.

When animals draw on their acting skills as a resource for self-defense or to obtain the necessities of life, they may be showing what researchers call a "theory of mind." This is the ability to actively consider what may be going on in *others'* minds, another being's thoughts about its own or other's thoughts. In human children, the theory of mind begins to emerge at around age two-and-a-half when they begin to reason about people's desires and emotions. In animals, no one knows for sure when—or even if—a theory of mind develops, though some species can certainly act as if they comprehend others' mental states, and they may use that capability as a resource to get along in the world, just as we do.

Grizzly bears, for instance, who surely seem to have ideas about a hunter's intentions, will find places to watch their pursuer without being seen. They have been observed using trees, bushes, or rocks as visual shields and also to make deliberate efforts to keep from leaving tracks that hunters could follow. Enos Mills, a noted conservationist, once described following a grizzly who turned and walked back on his own footprints several times to confuse his trail, then jumped into thick, scrubby underbrush that would hide his tracks.

Other animals seem to understand that people may have knowledge or abilities that the animals need, and they use that understanding, or theory of mind, as a resource to access the people's skills. When seeking assistance for solving a problem, animals will often go to great lengths to overcome their natural fear of people.

Len Howard describes just such an incident in her book *Birds as Individuals*. After she provided some wild birds with nesting boxes and food, the birds sometimes took treats from Howard's hand and visited her in her cottage. One day, a female blue titmouse flew inside making what Howard believed were urgent distress calls. Following the bird outside, Howard found that a cat had wrecked the tit's nest. Howard repaired the nest and replaced the bird's eggs, which soon hatched. The mother tit had been resourceful to seek assistance from Howard.

In *The Parrot's Lament*, Eugene Linden tells the beautiful story of Harriet, a leopard, who asked a favor from Indian conservationist Billy Arjan Singh. Singh had taken care of Harriet as a youngster, then released her in a preserve across the river from his home. The river flooded, and Harriet, presumably confident of Singh's kindness, carried her two cubs across the water to his kitchen, two floors above ground. After the water receded, she brought one cub back to her den. She must have decided that the river was still too dangerous for a second safe crossing because rather than swimming with her other cub, Harriet carried it to Singh's dugout canoe and waited until he figured out that she was hinting for help with transportation. Singh rowed her and the cub across the swiftly moving river.

Pepe, a male chimp at veterinarian Sheri Speede's primate rehabilitation center, once pointed out to her his injuries from a recent fight. Just in case she didn't take sufficient notice, he thrust his wounded leg out of his cage. Then he turned around to make sure she saw that his back was also injured. Speede obligingly flushed out his wounds with antiseptic.

Wup, an Airedale mix from Beaverton, Oregon, scratched and scratched at the entrance of his longtime veterinarian's clinic. When the doctor, William Ruggles, finally opened the door, he found Wup holding up a paw he'd cut on glass. Piglet, a Staffordshire bull terrier, once showed up badly limping at the Crofts Vet Practice in Blythe, Northumberland, England. The vet found that she'd slipped a disc, and from a microchip in her neck, the staff also discovered that Piglet had been a patient at the clinic *five* years earlier. After all that time, she'd managed to find the clinic again as a resource for help.

A cat named Tissue once sneaked into the waiting room of a veterinary hospital in Clacton, England. The staff repeatedly tried to put him out, but each time he managed to get back in.

Finally, the vet realized that Tissue was so determined to stay because he was having trouble breathing and desperately needed medical attention. Probably just hit by a car, this intelligent cat must have struck out on his own to find help at a place he had never visited before.

The most remarkable instance I've ever found of an animal seeking the resource of human assistance was reported in *Animal Citizen*, the official journal of the Indian government's Animal Welfare Board. One morning, at a veterinary clinic's outpatient ward, a monkey boldly walked straight through the lobby to the examining rooms. An attendant tried to shoo the monkey outside, but it attached itself to one of the veterinarian's feet and showed him a wound under its arm.

The doctor sedated the monkey and stitched up its cut; and when the animal came out of anesthesia, it got up off the operating table and left. For the next three days, though, it returned promptly at 8 A.M., allowed the vets to change its bandage, and then walked out again. On the fourth day, the monkey disappeared. Its cut must have healed enough that the animal no longer felt it needed help.

While these seem to be clear illustrations of animals calling on a theory of mind, it's difficult to determine exactly what animals might be thinking—and if their resourceful behavior is stemming from their ability to interpret the thoughts of other beings, or their ability to use other kinds of reasoning. Ola Sarefo, a guide at Botswana's Vumbura Camp, once saw a lion sauntering toward a warthog with feigned indifference while other lions in her pride, their bellies to the ground, hid hunched down in the grass surrounding the unsuspecting creature. Even though the female seemed unthreatening, as if she were just out for a casual afternoon stroll, the warthog still apparently preferred to move out of her way. In doing so, he walked straight into the ambush.

As those resourceful lions planned their hunt, did they have an idea of what the warthog would think about the female ambling toward him? Or did they only know, generally, that warthogs avoid lions, and then used that theory of behavior to predict their prey's reaction and carry out their hunt? We can't be sure. But University of Southern Louisiana psychologist Daniel Povinelli, who has done considerable research on theory of mind, says that "animals don't have to reason what the prey is thinking; they only have to reason about what it's going to do." And animals, like those lions, are surely excellent at it.

Povinelli also points out that "animals are good at detecting statistical regularities about how the world behaves." By detecting statistical regularities, such as what prey usually does when threatened, animals can analyze the information and apply their analysis as a resource for survival, in this case by carrying out a successful hunt. Some kinds of egrets may do this when going after fish. The birds run into shallow water to make the fish swim away to hide. Possibly with an understanding that fish regularly seek shady refuges, the egrets then form a canopy over their heads with their wings—and the fish swim straight under it to the resourceful egret's waiting beaks.

This kind of observing, analyzing, and predicting extends to inanimate objects as well as living things. Often animals come upon articles, like stones, theorize about their physical properties and possible "behavior," and use them as resources to improve their lives, for example by smashing open hard shells around nuts or mollusks. The articles become tools, which certain animals employ as extensions of themselves to get what they want.

Polar bears, for example, will throw chunks of ice to kill their prey, seals. The bears may pound rocks on ice to break through and catch seals swimming underneath. Black kites will swoop down on prey animals running for their lives from brushfires—

until the pickings get slim. Then the birds will throw smoldering sticks on a new spot to spread the flames and drive out more terrified animals. Crows are known to throw nuts on roads and wait for cars to come along and act as nutcrackers. Herons drop twigs, feathers, leaves, or berries into water as bait to attract fish. From the opposite perspective, archerfish use the water itself as a food-gathering tool, drawing it through their gills, then curling their tongues against the roofs of their mouths to make a little water-pistol barrel. When an insect flies over the water or lands on a low-hanging leaf, the fish will spit water at it with remarkably precise aim, knocking it down into their waiting mouths.

For self-protection, eagles, ravens, and other birds ward off enemies, including snakes and humans, by hitting them with stones. Some crab species will grab on to spiky sea urchins and hold them out in front of them as armor. An alley cat at Project Hope also used living things as tools. Another cat was chasing her, so she pulled back a rosebush branch with her paw and let the branch loose, thorns and all, to hit her enemy. She also was seen using the body of a sheep as a protective fort when a dog came after her. The cat dashed to the sheep, dug her claws into its belly, and hung upside down until the dog walked away. To save herself, this animal was surprisingly quick and inventive about taking advantage of objects that presented themselves.

Incredibly resourceful dogs and cats have used ordinary objects in their homes as tools, specifically tailored to help people they care about in a crisis. Perhaps an emergency situation forces animals to draw every bit of their resourcefulness out of themselves. Stress might encourage a clever action.

Jackie, a tabby-Abyssinian from Shawnee, Oklahoma, was devoted to all six children in her human family, but especially to four-year-old Benjamin, who suffered from asthma and sleep apnea. One night at 3 A.M., Benjamin's mother, Cindy Cluck, heard someone playing her piano. Strange, she thought, it must be one of the children. She got up and went into the living room, but instead of a child, she found Jackie stomping on the keys. The cat was also staring intently at the boys' bedroom; but when Cluck glanced in that direction, she saw no problem. She shooed Jackie off the piano.

The cat jumped back up and, again, batted the piano keys and looked toward the bedroom with her ears laid back flat. Finally, Cluck got the point: Jackie was trying to tell her to check on her sons. Cluck found Benjamin lying in bed, not breathing. If the cat hadn't been so resourceful, Cluck might not have gotten to the boy in time to save his life. Jackie had used the piano as a "tool" to get her attention.

One cold winter night, Scout, a Labrador retriever, saw his guardian, Mary Gladys Baker, fall and break her hip in her back-yard in Waurika, Oklahoma. Observing how vulnerable she was, Scout ran to his doghouse and got out an old quilt. He carried it to Baker in his teeth, covered her up, and cuddled next to her to comfort her and keep her warm until the next morning. Some-how he recognized that the blanket was just the "tool" he needed to help his beloved guardian.

Holly, a West Highland terrier from Cambridge, England, wit-nessed her guardian Roz Brown collapse, unconscious, in a dia-betic coma. So the dog climbed onto a table and got two pieces of candy that she herself had begged for, salivating, just a few hours earlier. Instead of eating the candy, however, Holly set it on the floor beside Brown's mouth. Brown regained consciousness and had just enough strength to eat the candy, which raised her blood sugar so that she could get to the kitchen for more substantial food. Holly's "tool" may have been intended to offer comfort, but it was, nevertheless, uncannily appropriate for saving Brown's life.

Trixie, a mixed-breed dog from Sydney, Australia, seemed to

understand that her guardian, Jack Fyfe, home alone and paralyzed after a stroke, desperately needed someone to bring him a drink of water. The dog soaked a towel in her water bowl, then dragged the towel to him and put it over his face so he could suck the moisture. For nine days, until his family happened to stop by the house, Trixie brought him water from her bowl and then from the toilet. Trixie, practically a canine genius, managed to keep her guardian from dying of dehydration.

Of course, not all animals are resourceful geniuses, any more than all people are. When it comes to cleverness, there can be significant differences among animals. This is clearly evident in orangutans, studied in Sumatra by Duke University biological anthropology professor Carel van Schaik.

One enterprising colony, he found, shoves sticks into natural indentations along the woody shell of neesia fruit to pry it open, then uses the stick to scrape away needly, stinging hairs around the seeds, which are full of nutritious oil. As the season progresses, the fruit—and the indentations in the shell—get larger. To accommodate, the orangs select thicker, stronger sticks to facilitate the prying and scraping. "The orangutans custom-make the tool according to their current need," says van Schaik. "Their tool is not a one-trick pony."

In sharp contrast to those smart animals are orangs in another colony, located on the far side of the river that the stick-users cannot ford. Those orangs are still in the habit of working with their teeth and limbs to break into the neesia shells and remove the seeds. So the orangs on one side of the river, apparently, are more resourceful than those on the other. Clearly, some animals figure out new ways to solve problems while others stumble on solutions by a lucky accident, then choose to continue to apply them. Some animals will both teach and learn willingly and ably. Still others don't do any of these things.

Resourcefulness can vary among groups of the same species, as it did among the Sumatran orangutans. But it can also vary among individuals within a group. How resourceful an animal turns out to be can hinge not just on ability but also on a willingness to be open to alternatives and new possibilities—and sometimes to put out effort to learn and find solutions to problems. Resourcefulness has much to do with choice.

If we give animals credit for their cleverness, which we can see with our own eyes, we must surely conclude that animals can choose to be resourceful and to adapt admirably in life. They can draw on their mental sharpness and physical skills to work around blizzards, droughts, illness, physical attacks, and other constant challenges that fate hands to them or those they love. Most animals' lives are full of tests, and animals regularly gather the resources to pass them.

8.

GENEROSITY

Recently a friend of mine was musing about her pet: "What does it take to keep a cat?" she asked. Just a little food and some kitty litter. Maybe one trip a year to the vet. "But, what a bargain," she added. "My cat asks so little, but she gives me back so much. She gives and gives and gives."

I understood exactly. In fact, over the years, dozens of animal lovers have made the same point to me. Though animals obviously can't give us literal presents wrapped in tissue paper and tied with floppy bows, they can, and do, give us emotional gifts in the form of love, support, concern, soothing, and companionship. Animals give these gifts through their actions, and they often do so freely, eagerly, and abundantly. When animals choose to give in this way, they demonstrate the virtue of generosity.

To explain what looks like animal generosity, scientists have developed theories, which I discussed in chapter 2 on compassion: reciprocal altruism (animals giving specifically to get something in return) and kin selection (animals giving to a relative solely to promote the survival of their genes). Yale University Professor Charles Brown, for example, discovered that cliff swallows will alert others in their colony to a swarm of insects they find. While they could be interpreted as generous sharing, in the same spirit as our invitations to friends to come over for a picnic, Brown explains that when a swallow recruits others, the bird does so only to increase the chance that together the colony can track the swarm's movement—giving the first bird more time to gobble down the insects. Clearly, Brown's interpretation stays far away from attributing a human motivation such as generosity to the swallows.

In addition to reciprocal altruism and kin selection, a third scientific explanation of what I view as animal generosity is instinctive behavior stemming from any animal's desire to protect its offspring. An example is Mollie, a beagle and dachshund mutt from Hainesport, Pennsylvania, who carried her pups, one by one, out of a ramshackle bungalow that went up in flames from a tipped-over kerosene heater. Bystanders saw Mollie's elderly guardian try to push her out a window to safety, but the dog fought and stayed inside. Then, as Mollie carried her pups out of the house into the snow, she was literally on fire. With flames flickering on her back and head, she kept making trips in and out of the house. Someone tried to throw a blanket over her to put out the flames, but Mollie resisted and ran back to her babies.

Finally, Mollie sat down in the snow with all six pups. Tufts of burned fur were hanging from her body. The tip of her nose and pads of her paws had been burned off. Her normally floppy ears were so injured and painful that she held them out, stiff. To save her puppies, this animal had sacrificed herself.

To me, this seems like a choice to be generous, though others might argue that Mollie was simply following maternal instinct, trying to extend her genes to future generations or ensuring the future reciprocity of pups who would grow up and protect and care for her.

Even if these motivations were at the root of Mollie's behavior, I would still call her generous because selfish motives don't always negate generosity. We all know, for example, that human parents can behave generously toward their child, while at the same time wanting to see part of themselves live on into the future through that child. Human parents also usually hope that their child will watch after them in their old age. For humans, instinct or selfish motives are not always mutually exclusive of generosity, and our behavior is often a complicated mix of all those things.

It's important to recognize that, regardless of complicated motives, animals can, and often do, choose to give generously of themselves. They choose whom to give to and whom not to give to—and whether to give to their family only, or to unrelated animals, or to members of an entirely different species. Says biologist Marc Bekoff, "Often animals will give whatever they have. They could be feeling that they're really doing something good."

What is it, exactly, that animals have to give? Well, for starters, food. Animals in the wild often share their much-needed food with others. Wolves regurgitate meat for pups in their pack, for instance. Vampire bats regurgitate blood into the mouths of others in their colonies. At the Yerkes Regional Primate Research Center, Frans de Waal once put two capuchin monkeys in adjacent cages with a wire mesh partition between them, then gave food to one, but not to the other. He conducted a total of eighteen tests with different combinations of monkeys. In every case, the animal who got food either handed, threw, or pushed some of it through the mesh to the one who had none.

A woman named Joanne Sweeny, from Columbia, Missouri, once observed similar behavior in her backyard. Her cat grabbed a sparrow, and Sweeny wrenched the bird from the cat's mouth and set it free. With its feathers greatly ruffled, the sparrow flew to the safety of a nearby fence. For the next hour, the bird's mate traveled back and forth to Sweeny's bird feeder and brought back seeds. Observes Sweeny, "The injured bird's mate was generous because he was likely hungry himself when he came to the feeder. But he ignored his needs to feed and comfort his distraught mate."

Johnny, a cat from Rockport, Massachusetts, may also have been generously trying to provide comfort with food. He lived with Frankie, a geriatric Labrador, who was too feeble to stand for long on his arthritic legs. The animals' guardian, Geoff Watson, kept finding Johnny's cat kibble all over the kitchen floor around Frankie's bed, and he assumed that the dog was knocking the cat's bowl off the counter to raid the food. But one day, Watson saw that generosity, not thievery, had been taking place in his kitchen: Watson witnessed Johnny batting his kibble across the floor to the less mobile Frankie, resting in his bed.

In Botswana, Peter and Beverly Pickford looked on as a honey badger used calls and movements to encourage another badger, with paralyzed legs, to drag itself over to a shady spot beneath tall grass. The healthy animal then caught a mouse, carried it back to the disabled badger, and proceeded to catch and donate the gift of a second mouse. The hunt took effort and energy, both of which were as willingly and generously offered to the needy badger as was the meal itself.

One of my favorite accounts of animals' generosity with food dates from World War II. The story concerns a wild monkey in the jungles of Sumatra and British sergeant Cyril Jones, who had been caught by his parachute in a tree. Somehow the animal must have recognized Jones's hunger and vulnerability, because for twelve straight days, this monkey searched for bananas and bamboo shoots and fed them to Jones. Even after Jones finally managed to cut himself free, the monkey accompanied him and continued to provide fruit as the sergeant wandered through the jungle to locate the rest of his division.

While some researchers might attribute animals' generosity with food as an attempt to impress onlookers in their social group, the monkey who shared food with Cyril Jones was clearly being generous to someone he perceived as needing help to stay alive. Chimpanzees who hand over a delicious treat are thought by some scientists to act out of a desire to enhance their status, power, popularity, or prestige. Males are thought to want to prove to female bystanders what good guys they are and thus how attractive they would be as mates. But Jones's monkey had no primate pals around him as he kept the strange human in the tree alive by sharing his own precious food resources.

It may be that animals share food not just because they're caring Good Samaritans, but also because they somehow feel responsible for others. At least that might be a plausible explanation for the generosity of Winnie, a boxer mutt, who took to roaming around her Raeford, North Carolina neighborhood and began to look extremely thin. Worried that Winnie's guardian had abandoned the dog and turned her loose to scrounge for food, a neighbor set out a bowl of dog food. The neighbor watched as Winnie, obviously starving, carefully picked up the bowl in her teeth and carried it across the street to her house. She set the bowl of food in front of the garage, then barked and yowled and ran in circles with great agitation. Two other neighbors opened the garage door and were outraged to see two golden retrievers trapped inside, close to death.

For a full month they'd been shut up in pitch blackness — and in summer temperatures over ninety degrees. The floor was covered with feces, urine, and piles of hair that the dogs had lost from malnourishment. Desperate for food and water, the dogs had pulled paint cans off the shelves and chewed them open. Broken teeth were scattered everywhere. Said one neighbor, "The dogs looked like victims of a concentration camp."

Apparently, Winnie had known about the goldens' misery and desperation and had probably been trying to figure out a way to help them. Kim Shelton, a Humane Society cruelty investigation officer, noted that Winnie, though hungry herself, "sacrificed the food she was given in order to feed the other dogs." Canids are said instinctively to watch after their pack, and Winnie may very well have acted out of a sense of duty. She showed exquisite generosity, making her, in Shelton's words, "clearly a hero."

Animals also show great generosity with food from their own bodies. In Massachusetts, a pregnant goat named Belle was rescued after escaping from a slaughterhouse truck. She was stressed and sick and thin but still managed to give birth to two healthy bucks. She immediately went into shock from calcium depletion; and though she desperately needed to lie down and rest, she struggled to her feet and stood on wobbly legs to nurse the bucks. She nursed them, in fact, for the next two *years* until they towered over her and had to lower themselves to their knees to get to her teats. Says Meg Randa, who adopted Belle, "She was incredibly giving of herself."

Domestic and wild animals often foster not just their own kind, but also babies of a completely different species. One generous horse, Maraja, from Mellen, Wisconsin, nursed a calf, who had been rejected by its mother. A goat from Harrisonburg, Virginia, was seen to climb on a stool, then stand on a table, so an orphaned foal could nurse from her.

Cats and dogs can be so willing to care for another's babies that they're often kept just for that purpose at zoos, shelters, and

animal rehabilitation centers. Cats have been known to nurse orphaned rabbits, squirrels, and hedgehogs, and dogs are reported
to have fostered needy possums, fawns, lions, and bears. One
dog, a Yorkie named Two Bits from Brownwood, Texas, once
took over the litter of a cat named Scroungie, who had lived in the
same house and who was killed by a car shortly after giving birth.
A mangy, starving stray dog named Emmy was found along the
side of a road in Cape Town, South Africa. She was nursing two
orphaned kittens.

Though male animals can't literally nurse and provide milk,
they also often seem to show great concern when caring for others' offspring. I've read of a male cardinal who, for four months,
brought food to goldfish in a lily pond and fed them, beak to
mouth. A male Siamese cat in Russia took care of several baby
chicks, brought home by his guardian, Galina Samoilova. The
cat would lie down beside the chicks and embrace them with his
paws as they crawled under him as if he were their mother. Sti-
fling whatever natural inclination he might have had to kill birds,
this cat instead chose generously to sleep with the chicks, cuddle
them, and protect them.

At just six months of age, Barney, a male cocker spaniel,
started watching after puppies for his guardian, Elaine Jewell,
who takes in orphaned, hurt, and abused pups for her rescue
work in Preston, Mississippi. "I bottle-feed them, and Barney
does the rest," Jewell says. He warms, cleans, and snuggles with
the babies. And he actually tries to feed them by lying down and
letting them suckle rolls of fat on his chest. He generously does
this until his chest is bald and red and sore.

According to American University biologist Cathy Schaeff
who studies harbor seals, it is instinct or hormones that drives
mother animals to take care of an orphaned baby, especially if
their own baby has died but they are still physically primed for

nursing. "A female seal who has the hormones to care for a pup but not the infant itself will try to foster any pup she can find," Schaeff says. She speculates that by taking on another's baby, the mother will gain experience that may help her be a better mother the next time around; so fostering could increase the odds that her future offspring will survive. Harbor seals in particular may nurse others' babies simply because they are, says Schaeff, "bad at recognizing their own pups." When a mother harbor seal returns from feeding, she may nurse several different pups beside her own, even if her own is just a few feet away. Biologist Marc Bekoff, on the other hand, while agreeing that fostering might be driven in part by instinct or hormones, suggests that animals who foster do so, perhaps, "just because they see a baby animal in need and want to help. That helping is generous."

When animals care for others' babies, they offer not just food from their bodies, but also their time and energy—in the form of affection, concern, and support. When animals support others, they are being generous.

Sometimes, their support is literal and physical. Sam, a St. Bernard, was romping in the Susquehanna River with his guardian, Kathi Zerance, when she suffered a sudden brain aneurysm and sank below the water's surface. Sam swam to her. He kept Zerance afloat for half an hour, until he was able to scramble onto a rock and pull her ashore.

While stories of physical support like Sam's abound, there are equally limitless examples of generous animals providing emotional and psychological support. One such account involves Roscoe, a white German shepherd from Omaha, Nebraska, who was inseparable friends with a neighborhood dog named Buster. One day as the two roamed a local nature preserve, Buster chased a possum to the end of a twenty-foot drainage tube that dropped off into a pit of freezing cold water. Buster was unable to get out of the pit; and as he tried frantically to stay afloat, Roscoe ran two miles to get help. Then he came straight back to his friend.

Seeming to have the demeanor of people who stay close by friends in a crisis to buoy their spirits, Roscoe was found lying on a ledge above the opening of the culvert where Buster was trapped. The dog's rescuers noticed that Roscoe refused to budge until a fireman wriggled through the drainage tube, got a rope around Buster, and pulled him to safety.

Katrina, a beagle and Jack Russell mix, was brought to Project Hope. The dog had been rescued from a ten-foot-square pen, where she had lived all her life with little food and water and no shade in temperatures that often reached over a hundred degrees.

At the sanctuary, Katrina observed a puppy named Freckles who was listlessly lying around. Afflicted with a bad case of bronchitis, Freckles had to stay inside alone when the other dogs were let outside to play. Clearly understanding the hardship of suffering in isolation, for several days Katrina came quietly to the pup's bed, snuggled up to her and licked her, as if she were trying to raise her spirits.

Katrina's generous actions were, in a dog way, not so different from our own when we take the time and energy to go and see a friend in the hospital. Like Katrina, we lend emotional support by visiting because we want to help and give what we can.

As a kitten, China, a cat from Jamestown, New York, "adopted" a little stuffed dolphin and for years would sleep cuddled up to it every night, with her paw draped over the toy's dorsal fin. She would lick the dolphin's plush fur clean, drag the dolphin with her everywhere, and bring it to her food dish, as cats may do with cherished possessions.

But this stuffed animal was more than a beloved toy to China; it was her security blanket. And one afternoon, when China's guardian, Carol Butcher, was crying, overwhelmed by the strain of the divorce she was undergoing, China sat at Butcher's feet and watched until she fell asleep on her bed. When Butcher woke, she felt something soft and fuzzy on her face. It was China's toy dolphin, which the cat had brought to her as she slept.

Most of us have made casseroles to offer to grieving friends. We've sent flowers to cheer up sick people or cards to give support to those we love who are downtrodden. Says Butcher, "China knew I needed comforting. She did the only thing she could for me—she brought me her *own* comfort."

Chuckles, a large, shaggy black dog, was known for putting prized possessions in his toy box. His guardian, Heather Ramoff, had to warn houseguests not to leave their suitcases open because Chuckles would steal their socks and store them away. Interviewed for a Discovery Channel documentary, "Pet Love," she says, "Once they were in his toy box, as far as he was concerned, those items were his."

Ramoff was recovering from surgery from ovarian cancer, and one day, feeling weak and ill, she lay down on the sofa to take a nap. When she awoke, Chuckles had carefully arranged all of his precious toys around her body. "His little yellow ducky was under my chin. His rabbit was stuffed behind my head. A frisbee was on my stomach; a stuffed squirrel, somewhere else. Tennis balls were everywhere," says Ramoff. "I wasn't sure what it meant. But in the end, I decided that he was just giving me everything he had. He was giving his all."

The generous concern of animals will sometimes extend so far as one creature's sacrificing its own well-being for another's. Even the simplest of creatures can do this, in fact. Pea aphids, when infected by parasitic wasp larvae, will commit suicide so as not to expose their brothers and sisters to the larvae. Bruce Waldman, a Harvard biologist, observed that in a brood of tadpoles, the runts will refrain from competing with their healthier siblings for food: At possible costs to themselves, the weaker tadpoles give the stronger ones a better chance to develop into frogs. Regardless of how conscious these self-sacrificing choices are, they do demonstrate some kind of generous impulse.

Generosity is more obvious and surely more consciously chosen in animals who have brains of greater complexity and still decide to put themselves out on behalf of others. In these cases, the animals may be giving willingly of themselves just for the sake of doing good.

James Porter, an oceanographer, wrote in *Oceans* about an incident off the Florida coast, where he saw a pod of thirty whales surrounding an elderly male. The male was lying on his side in shallow water with blood seeping from his right ear, which was infested with parasitic worms. Although he was positioned so that he could breathe without having to work to swim to the water's surface, his blowhole would be occasionally submerged, forcing him to struggle for air. Clearly, the whale was dying.

But not alone. On each side of him fourteen or fifteen whales formed a wedge and kept pressing toward him to support him. Porter tried three times to snorkel toward the old male, but each time a member of the pod would leave the others, slide its head underneath Porter, and transport him to the beach away from the sick friend. Porter watched as the whales whipped their tails and churned the water to drive away a lurking shark. Personnel from the U.S. Coast Guard and National Park Service arrived on the scene and tried to separate the whales, but nothing could stop them from regrouping, tightly packed, around the dying male.

These whales had put themselves at risk by staying so close to shore through shifting tides. They also sacrificed their health and comfort: As the sun beat down on them, it burned their backs, which were exposed in the shallow water. Though any of the whales could have left at any time, they generously chose to remain as a group until the old male died.

Sadie, an English setter from Bethpage, Tennessee, demonstrated the same kind of generous protectiveness. While on a walk, Sadie's guardian, Michael Miller, suddenly felt his pulse pounding and his wrist throbbing with horrible pain. He attached Sadie's leash from his belt loop to her collar, so they could start home. But then he collapsed to the ground. Miller had suffered a massive heart attack.

Sadie and Michael Miller

Sadie licked her guardian's cheeks and whined, but she could not rouse him. So she started pulling with all her might to get him home. Sadie, you must realize, weighed just 45 pounds. Miller weighed 180. For an hour and a half, as Miller slipped in and out of consciousness, the dog would tug and yank his body, then come back and lick his face, then tug and yank some more. After dragging him a third of a mile up and down hills, Sadie got Miller to his back door. There, she barked and howled until his wife came out and took Miller to the hospital.

It's easy to imagine how hard Sadie had to work and how much she surely stressed every bone, muscle, and ligament in her body. Her generous sacrifice is obvious, as was the sacrifice of Holly, an elderly springer spaniel from British Columbia. One day Holly's guardian, Norma Myers, was walking with her granddaughter Ally along the Similkameen River when suddenly a doe ran out of the woods and raced straight toward Ally. Holly jumped between the two and bit the deer's leg. Holly ended up with bruises, a broken leg, and an irreparably damaged eye.

It's likely Holly got into the fight without an understanding of the sacrifice of pain she was about to make. Still, this doesn't negate the generosity of her decision to offer protection against an animal so much larger than she. As the doe loomed over her, Holly surely knew she was in danger, yet she nevertheless forged ahead to protect Ally.

Attie, a monkey at South Africa's Vervet Monkey Founda-

Holly and Ally

tion, chose to help his friend Luke, even knowing he was going to suffer pain for doing it. Luke had gone to visit a female in a nearby enclosure, but in order to get there, he had climbed over an electric fence. Luke then wanted to come back to his own family and friends, but he was afraid of getting shocked again when he returned over the fence.

As Luke stood by the fence, clearly distressed, Attie apparently decided to come to the rescue. Knowing full well he was about to be shocked—twice—he climbed over the fence to reach his friend. Luckily, the foundation's director, Arthur Hunt, arrived and turned off the electricity just as Attie was about to lead Luke back over the fence to their enclosure and get the second shock.

Many animals have taken generous self-sacrifice beyond the experience of pain to death. In Greenbrier, Arkansas, a miniature Chihuahua named Lady Bug assaulted a two-hundred-pound rottweiler who was attacking a toddler. To protect the girl, this tiny dog generously took on an opponent she had to have known could mean the end of her. Sadly, Lady Bug died during her valiant fight—but the little girl survived unscathed.

Missy, a Belgian shepherd from Chicago, once ran across an alley and shoved Dashun McMiller, age six, into the arms of his stepfather—just as an oncoming car hit the place where the boy had been. Missy was killed instantly. Lady, a rottweiler-Alsatian from England, threw herself in front of a motorcycle that was hurtling toward eighteen-month-old Kathryn Dias. Kathryn was saved, but Lady was killed. The driver roared off without a backward glance.

Robin Eckel, an officer in New Jersey's Monmouth County Sheriff's Department, told me of the amazing sacrifice of his German shepherd police dog, Solo. One morning, around 2 A.M., the pair was called to break up a standoff between police and an

Solo

armed robber who was believed to be hiding on the second floor of an apartment building. All the tenants had been evacuated; and for almost twelve hours, the police had been waiting for the man to come out. They were starting to wonder if the robber was in the apartment at all.

When Eckel and Solo arrived, Eckel shouted to the man that if he didn't come out, the police were going to send a dog in after him. Though in these situations a few dog barks usually encourage suspects to surrender, there was no response from the robber. At 5 A.M., the decision was made to send in Solo, who would find and grab the robber, and then the police would quickly follow.

Although dispatching a dog is a typical step in a standoff, Eckel felt apprehensive as he watched his dog go up the building's stairs. Solo must have surely felt the tension of the situation. According to Eckels, the dog had an amazingly clear understanding of danger — but he still chose to continue on.

Solo turned a corner out of sight and started down the hall

toward the apartment where the robber was supposed to be. Eckel heard a gunshot, then another one. Then silence. For the next five hours, while the standoff continued, Eckel agonized over the fate of his dog.

"My heart didn't want to believe he was dead," Eckels says. "I kept thinking, 'I've got to get him to the vet.' " But when the robber finally surrendered, Eckel was allowed to go into the apartment, where he learned that one of the two bullets had killed Solo.

"There's no doubt of Solo's generosity and sacrifice," Eckel told me later. "He would do anything for me. He gave two hundred percent all the time." In this situation, Solo was surely aware of the danger, and he was no puppet. He made a choice to do as he was asked. And, certainly, the choice was a generous one. Eckel believes that Solo made it out of love for him.

Some people might say that Solo was just blindly acting on instinct to serve and protect Eckel, the "alpha male" of his "pack." In my opinion, it seems clear that Solo had a big heart and he knew full well what he was doing. Says biologist Marc Bekoff, when animals give of themselves and sacrifice for us, "they show unconditional love and trust and devotion. They can't let you be in danger. They make choices to help."

Humans demonstrate generosity through self-sacrifice as well. Policemen and firemen put themselves willingly in the line of danger; doctors and nurses give time, energy, and strength to attend to the sick; almost every day people offer whatever talent they have to serve, inspire, or care for those they love or even those they barely know. But perhaps the most common way we have of demonstrating generosity is through giving thanks—to those policemen and firemen who save us, the doctors and nurses who make us well, or the people who give of themselves for our well-being.

Though it's impossible to tell if animals feel gratitude, I believe that they, like us, can be generous with their thanks. Certainly, behavior that might be seen as an expression of thanks can be ambiguous: When we feed a dog and it jumps around, whimpering and wagging its tail, the dog may be showing excitement or gratitude, or maybe both. Our interpretation hinges on whether we are willing to give animals credit for feeling grateful and wanting us to know it.

That might be too much of a stretch for most animal behaviorists, but Bekoff, for one, believes that "animals are absolutely capable of gratitude." As an example, he told me about Jethro, his own dog, who generously showed his gratitude to Bekoff for rescuing him from the pound. Jethro plastered himself to his new guardian and followed him around, nonstop.

Says Bekoff, "If you adopt animals, they're grateful." Some recently adopted animals have been known to give generous thanks by trying hard to help their new human families. On the very first night after being brought to a new home, a number of animals have warned of fires, for instance, or have confronted criminals. Just a few days after being adopted, a dog named Ai Go, fought off a burglar who attacked his guardian in her Bangkok shoe shop. On his first night after coming to live in his new home, Teddy, a German shepherd from Utah, paced around his new guardians' bedroom until they woke and went to the kitchen. On the table they found a crowbar, left by a burglar who had used the tool to force open the kitchen window before Teddy ran him off.

These dogs' helping their new families so soon after adoption may have been a fluke of no significance. Or it may have been an example of reciprocal altruism; the dogs could be said to be returning the favor of being given a home. Just as likely, their helping was their way of showing gratitude, not just loyalty or protectiveness, because the animals were offering

Scooter and Fred Priest

help long before they could have bonded with their new guardians or come to feel that they belonged with them.

Fred Priest of Belmont, Nova Scotia, feels without question that Scooter, a German shepherd mongrel he adopted, felt gratitude. Scooter had experienced a rough life: Her previous guardians had neglected her, and she had been the victim of abuse. Even when taken into a safe home, Scooter would cower at certain things, like the cane of Priest's mother. The dog was also particularly frightened of men.

She was never scared of Priest, however. Even on their initial ride home, she seemed to show her gratitude to him for giving her a loving home. She jumped on his lap and licked him and seemed to whine her thanks for the entire thirty-minute trip. "I think she knew the minute I put her in the van that I loved dogs and would be nice to her. She knew she was getting a good life," Priest says.

Soon afterward, he believes, she even more generously thanked him for providing it. On a blustery, winter afternoon, as the temperature dipped to minus-thirty degrees, Priest took Scooter for a walk. Because she was so new to his farm, he kept her on a lead of heavy nylon cord to prevent her from wandering away and getting lost.

As he started to walk a frozen river on his property, the ice suddenly cracked. Priest crashed into water cold enough to kill him in minutes. The water also was dangerously deep. He tried to grab the ice, but it was too slippery for a grip. Clutching Scooter's lead, Priest says, "was all I had. It was like a lifeline."

Scooter seemed to know it. Instead of barking excitedly or coming closer to investigate, as dogs might do, she stood exactly where she was. The instant Priest tried to climb up the nylon cord attached to her, she dug her nails into the ice to hold herself in place. In his sodden winter coat, Priest weighed at least two hundred pounds, and Scooter, only fifty-five. Still, she braced herself until he climbed to safety. Priest believes she tried so hard to help him out of "love and gratitude for someone who had so recently taken her in." With great and generous effort, she may well have been trying to thank him.

Animals also give thanks with more subtle gestures. Ontario policeman Dan Robertson tells of a two-month-old puppy who got tangled in a phone cord. Choking and fighting to free herself, she inadvertently pressed the telephone's "0" and got connected to an operator. The call was traced; and after Robertson broke into the house and set the pup free, "she began bounding all over the living room," he says, "and kissing me in appreciation."

A stray cat, fed by Margaret Thornton of Fort Worth, Texas, tried in her cat way to give generous thanks. For four years she'd eaten whatever Thornton set out for her, but she'd barely let Thornton touch her. Then one summer night, as Thornton sat on her back steps, the cat surprisingly climbed into her lap, put her paws on Thornton's shoulders, nuzzled her neck, and purred. The next day, a car hit the cat and killed her. "I've wondered ever since if she had some sixth sense that her end was near, and she came to thank me for taking care of her and feeding her," Thornton says. Even if the cat had no sense of what lay ahead of her, she had chosen to stop being standoffish. Her loving behavior may have been a generous, quiet expression of gratitude.

At his veterinary clinic, William Ruggles once saved the life of a Boston bulldog, who was suffering from strychnine poisoning. A few weeks later, the dog was back, scratching at Ruggles's door. When the vet opened it, the dog leapt up and licked his hands. Says Ruggles, "I could tell that what I had done for the dog was gratefully appreciated."

Frank McCubbins had a similar experience with an appreciative dog in Sweet Home, Oregon. As McCubbins milked his cows one Sunday morning, he heard pathetic moaning outside his barn and went to investigate. Huddled next to a fence was a little brown mutt, who raised his hackles, curled his lip, and snarled as McCubbins sat beside him. McCubbins discovered that a cable snare set for coyotes was slowly strangling the dog. The harder the animal tried to free himself, the tighter the cable cut, like a noose, into his flesh.

McCubbins carefully released the dog, and he took a couple of cautious steps, then, with ears flying, shot across the pasture. Then he stopped, turned around, ran back, and threw himself in a flying leap against McCubbins's chest. He wiggled his body, wagged his tail, and licked McCubbins's entire face. After a few minutes, the dog suddenly took off again. "I can't think of any other reason why he came back like that except to thank me," McCubbins says.

When rescued, even wild animals can be generous about showing their appreciation. In South Africa, Stephanie Wolf had saved a little baboon named Chewie. Every day after she dressed his wounds, Chewy would reach up and put his hand on her cheek, "like a thank you," Wolf says. Ann Van Dyk got a similar impression from a cheetah living at her wildlife sanctuary. During a storm that pelted down hailstones as big as golf balls, Van Dyk became worried about her young cheetahs and hurried to their enclosure. She found a male who had panicked in the storm and had exhausted himself in his struggle to run away—anywhere. Van Dyk carried him to a warm bed in her hospital and rubbed him down with a towel. She says, "He slowly started to purr and then to lick my hand in gratitude."

In *Cruising World*, Mark and Caron D'Ambroso describe a sailing trip through Venezuela's Los Roques Islands, where they found a dolphin whose tail had been caught in a fishnet. A white nylon cord was cutting into her flukes. Unable to escape these traps, she was breathing hard and calling, "Wee-aht! Wee-aht!" as if for help. Mark and Caron cautiously approached the dolphin and cut her free.

The next morning, the dolphin appeared again. She swam around the boat once and then disappeared. A while later, Caron found someone's winch handle lying in their dinghy. She had no idea how it had gotten there; but she and Mark soon figured out the mystery when the dolphin returned and dropped a green glass bottle in the dinghy, too. Caron and Mark applauded, and the dolphin, whom they named Scraps, must have understood that they liked her gifts. She came back with a plastic sandal, another bottle, a coffee mug, a length of pipe, and two aluminum cans. Mark and Caron got the message: Scraps was probably saying dolphin words of "thanks" for their rescue.

In addition to animals who demonstrate generosity in these specific ways, there are some animals who just seem to embody generosity. It radiates from them as if it were embedded in their spirit. Those of you who love animals know exactly the type I mean. These creatures are like the people whom Italians call "a piece of bread," meaning that they're soft, pliable, easy-going, and nourishing with their generous natures. And the perfect example of this kind of animal is Jessie, a Labrador retriever who lived with Beverly and Rudy Herrera in San Leandro, California.

All Jessie seemed to *do* in life was give. This dog behaved as though giving was her reason for being set down on the earth. Every day, say her guardians, she gave them love, kindness, support, protection, devotion, and comfort. And she gave these things abundantly.

One autumn, Rudy's sister died. Beverly stayed home with him for several days, but then she had to go back to work. On her way out the door, she took Jessie's face in her hands and looked into her big brown eyes. "Take care of Daddy today. Don't let him be sad," she said to the dog.

Jessie must have responded to this request with the earnestness of a human taking an oath on a Bible. For the whole day, she stuck like lint to Rudy. Instead of lying in the hall while he showered, as she usually did, she went into the bathroom and leaned against the tub. Instead of curling up at his feet when he sat down, she sat next to him and watched him intently. In fact, all day she never took her eyes off him. If he got up, she got up. If he walked into another room, she followed him with her nose pressed against his leg. Only when Beverly came home did Jessie go off duty. With an exhausted sigh, she lay down on her bed and fell asleep.

Years later when Jessie was dying of cancer and was too sick even to stand, Rudy slept on the floor beside her on her last night. As weak as she was, she struggled to raise herself on her front legs and lean against him. Ruby believes Jessie was trying to comfort him in his grief about her illness and approaching death. Again, seeming to think only of him and not herself, she wanted to support him and boost his spirits.

The next morning, Beverly took over and curled up on the floor around Jessie. By then, the dog couldn't even lift her head. But she kept turning it and pushing it against Beverly's cheek, as if she were giving whatever strength she had left to offer love. Beverly believes that in Jessie's physically limited way, she was trying to "hug" her good-bye. Says Beverly, "She was trying to help me through all my sadness. But it was more, too. She was trying to thank me for being with her and helping her, and for all our years of love and friendship."

Skeptics might say that Beverly was projecting her own feelings onto Jessie: The dog wasn't the one giving and thanking; it was Beverly herself. Jessie just wanted petting and reassurance as she faded away in her last hours.

But the interpretation of that beautiful moment between Jessie and Beverly depends on how you want to look at it—and how you want to see so much of what animals do all around us. I believe that Jessie was choosing to do good, just like the other animals in this book. She was making that choice all the way to the very end of her life.

As Jessie pressed her face against Beverly's cheek, no neon sign was there to point out the importance of what was taking place. Yet that subtle gesture says everything we need to know about Jessie—and all animals'—potential for generosity. It speaks volumes about animals' loyalty, sensitivity, concern for others' welfare, and great capacity for love. In moments like that one, we can see all the beauty that so many animals choose to show us.

SELECTED
BIBLIOGRAPHY

Adcock, Fleur, and Jacqueline Simms, eds. 1995. *Oxford Book of Creatures*. Oxford: Oxford University Press.

Allaby, Michael. 1982. *Animal Artisans*. New York: Knopf.

Barber, Theodore Xenophon. 1993. *The Human Nature of Birds*. New York: St. Martin's.

Barnett, John L., Paul H. Hemsworth, and R. Bryan Jones. 1993. Behavioural responses of commercially farmed laying hens to humans: Evidence of stimulus generalization. *Applied Animal Behaviour Science* 37 (2): 139–146.

Baun, Mara M., Nancy Bergstrom, Nancy F. Langston, and Linda Thoma. 1984. Physiological effects of human/companion animal bonding. *Nursing Research* 33 (3): 126–129.

Beck, Alan, and Aaron Katcher. 1996. *Between Pets and People: The Importance of Animal Companionship*. Indiana: Purdue University Press.

Brown, Charles R., Mary B. Brown, and Martin L. Shaffer. 1991. Food-sharing signals among socially foraging cliff swallows. *Animal Behaviour* 42 (4): 551–564.

Buck, Ross. 1997. *Communicative Genes and the Evolution of Empathy*. New York: The Guilford Press.

Budiansky, Stephen. 1997. *The Nature of Horses: Exploring Equine Evolution, Intelligence, and Behavior*. New York: The Free Press.

Burnam, John C. 2000. *Dog Tags of Courage: The Turmoil of War and the Rewards of Companionship*. Fort Bragg, CA: Lost Coast Press.

Campbell, Andrea. 1999. *Bringing Up Ziggy*. Los Angeles: Renaissance Books.

Caras, Roger. 1990. *A Cat Is Watching: A Look at the Way Cats See Us*. Boston: G. K. Hall & Co.

———. 1992. *A Dog Is Listening: The Way Some of Our Closest Friends View Us*. New York: Summit Books.

———. 1996. *A Perfect Harmony: The Intertwining Lives of Animals and Humans Throughout History*. New York: Simon & Schuster.

Danguir, J., and S. Nicolaidis. 1975. Protection of a naïve rat from drinking a solution by rats who have learned to refuse it. *C.R. Hebd. Séances Acad. Sci.*, Serie D, 280 (22): 2595–2598.

Darwin, Charles. 1872. *The Expression of the Emotions in Man and Animals*. Reprint, Chicago and London: The University of Chicago Press, 1965.

Davis, Hank, and Dianne Balfour. 1992. *The Inevitable Bond: Examining Scientist-Animal Interactions*. Cambridge: Cambridge University Press.

Dawkins, R. 1976. *The Selfish Gene*. Oxford: Oxford University Press.

de Waal, Frans. 1996. *Good Natured: The Origins of Right and Wrong in Humans and Other Animals*. Cambridge, MA: Harvard Press.

———, Lesleigh M. Luttrell, and M. Eloise Canfield. 1993. Preliminary data on voluntary food sharing in brown capuchin monkeys. *American Journal of Primatology* 29 (1): 73–78.

Dodman, Nicholas. 1996. *The Dog Who Loved Too Much: Tales, Treatments, and the Psychology of Dogs*. New York: Bantam Books.

———. 1997. *The Cat Who Cried for Help: Attitudes, Emotions, and the Psychology of Cats*. New York: Bantam Books.

Dossey, L. 1997. The healing power of pets: A look at animal-assisted therapy. *Alternative Therapies* 3: 8–15.

Dugatkin, Lee. 1999. *Cheating Monkeys and Citizen Bees: The Nature of Cooperation in Animals and Humans*. New York: Free Press.

Durrell, Gerald Malcom. 1979. *My Family and Other Animals*. New York: Viking.

Estes, Richard Despard. 1991. *The Behavior Guide to African Mammals*. Halfway House, South Africa: Russel Friedman Books CC.

Flicken, Millicent. 1981. Food finding in black-capped chickadees: Altruistic communication? *The Wilson Bulletin* 93 (3): 393–394.

Garber, Marjorie. 1996. *Dog Love*. New York: Simon & Schuster.

Gonzales, Philip, and Leonore Fleischer. 1995. *The Dog Who Rescues Cats: The True Story of Ginny*. New York: HarperCollins.

Grandin, Temple. 1995. *Thinking in Pictures*. New York: Doubleday.

Greene, David. 1986. *Your Incredible Cat*. Garden City, NY: Doubleday & Company.

Griffin, Donald. 1984. *Animal Thinking*. Cambridge: Harvard University Press.

———. 1992. *Animal Minds*. Chicago: University of Chicago Press.

Hall-Martin, Anthony. 1993. *A Day in the Life of an African Elephant*. Halfway House: Southern Book Publishers Ltd.

Heinrich, Bernd. 1999. *Mind of the Raven*. New York: Cliff Street Books.

Holldobbler, Bert, and Edward O. Wilson. 1990. *The Ants*. Cambridge, MA: Harvard University Press.

Howard, L. 1953. *Birds as Individuals*. London: Readers Union, Collins.

Insel, Thomas R. 1993. Oxytocin and the neuroendocrine basis of affiliation. In *Hormonally Induced Changes in Mind and Brain*, 225–251. San Diego: Academic Press, Inc.

———. 1997. A neurobiological basis of social attachment. *American Journal of Psychiatry* 154 (6): 726–735.

Irwin, Bill. 1992. *Blind Courage: A 2,000 Mile Journey of Faith*. Los Angeles:WRS Publishers.

Lasher, Margot. 1996. *And the Animals Will Teach You*. New York: Berkeley Books.

———. 1998. A relational approach to the human-animal bond. *Anthrozoos* 11 (3): 130–133.

Lemish, G. H. 1996. *War Dogs: Canines in Combat*. Washington, D.C.: Brassey.

Leslie, Robert. 1968. *The Bears and I*. New York: Dutton.

Limbaugh, C. 1961. Cleaning Symbiosis. *Scientific American*.

Linden, Eugene. 1999. *The Parrot's Lament: And Other Tales of Animal Intrigue, Intelligence, and Ingenuity*. New York: Dutton.

Lund, Jorgen Damkjer, and Mads Jorgensen. 1999. Behaviour patterns and time course of activity in dogs with separation problems. *Applied Animal Behaviour Science* 63 (3): 219–236.

Luttman, Rick, and Gail Luttman. 1976. *Chickens in Your Backyard*. Emmaus, PA: Rodale Press, Inc.

Masserman, Jules H., Stanley Wechkin, and William Terris. 1964. "Altruistic" behavior in rhesus monkeys. American Psychiatric Association 120th Annual Meeting, Los Angeles.

———. 1977. *Dogs Never Lie About Love*. New York: Crown Publishers.

Masson, Jeffrey. 1995. *When Elephants Weep*. New York: Delacorte.

McCormick, A., and D. McCormick. 1997. *Horse Sense and the Human Heart*. Deerfield Beach, FL: Health Communications.

McElroy, Susan Chernak. 1996. *Animals as Teachers & Healers*. New York: Ballantine.

————. 1998. *Animals as Guides for the Soul*. New York: Ballantine.

McFarland, David, ed. 1981. *The Oxford Companion to Animal Behaviour*. Oxford: Oxford University Press.

McKinney, William T. 1986. Primate separation studies: Relevance to bereavement. *Psychiatric Annals* 16 (5): 281–287.

Mendoza, Sally P., and William A. Mason. 1997. Attachment relationships in New World primates. In *The Integrative Neurobiology of Affiliation*, 203–209.

Mitchelle, Robert W., Nicholas S. Thompson, and H. Lyn Miles, eds. 1997. *Anthropomorphism, Anecdotes, and Animals*. Albany, NY: SUNY Press.

Morgan, Paul B. 1999. *K-9 Soldiers: Vietnam and After*. Central Point, OR: Hellgate Press.

Moss, Cynthia. 1988. *Elephant Memories: Thirteen Years in the Life of an Elephant Family*. New York: William Morrow and Co.

Nordquist, Charles. 1985. Killer whale shares food with gulls at the Vancouver Public Aquarium. *Zoo Biology* 4 (4): 367–374.

O'Connell, Sanjida. 1995. Empathy in chimpanzees: Evidence for theory of mind? *Primates* 36 (3): 397–410.

Page, George. 1999. *In Search of the Animal Mind*. New York: Doubleday.

Palombit, Ryne A., Robert M. Seyfarth, and Dorothy L. Cheney. 1997. The adaptive value of "friendships" to female baboons: Experimental and observational evidence. *Animal Behavior* 54: 599–614.

Patterson, Francine, and Eugene Linden. 1981. *The Education of Koko*. New York: Holt, Rinehart & Winston.

Paulsen, Gary. 1994. *Winterdance: The Fine Madness of Running the Iditarod*. New York: Harcourt Brace.

Payne, Katy. 1998. *Silent Thunder: In the Presence of Elephants*. New York: Simon & Schuster.

Pellis, Sergio M., Vivien C. Pellis, and Mario M. McKenna. 1993. Some subordinates are more equal that others: Play fighting amongst adult subordinate male rats. *Aggressive Behavior* 19 (5): 385–393.

Peterson, B., D. Metzger, and L. Hogan, eds. 1998. *Intimate Nature: The Bond between Woman and Animals*. New York: Ballantine.

Porter, J. W. 1977. Pseudorca stranding. *Oceans* 4: 8–14.

Povinelli, Daniel J., Kurt E. Nelson, and Sarah T. Boysen. 1992. Comprehension of role reversal in chimpanzees: Evidence of empathy? *Animal Behaviour* 43 (4): 633–640.

Premack, David, and Ann James Premack. 1984. *The Mind of an Ape*. New York: W. W. Norton.

Pryor, Karen. 1995. *On Behavior*. North Bend, WA: Sunshine.

Rasa, O. Anne. 1983. Dwarf mongoose and hornbill mutualism in the Taru Desert, Kenya. *Behavioral Ecology and Sociobiology* 12 (3): 181–190.

Reinhardt, Viktor, and Annie Reinhardt. 1981. Cohesive relationships in a cattle herd. *Behaviour* 77 (3): 121–151.

Rhine, J. B. 1951. The present outlook on the question of psi in animals. *Journal of Parapsychology* 15: 230–251.

Rhine, J. B., and S. R. Feather. 1962. The study of cases of psi-trailing in animals. *Journal of Parapsychology* 16: 1–22.

Ridley, M. 1996. *The Origins of Virtue*. London: Viking.

Ruckert, Janet. 1987. *The Four-Footed Therapist*. Berkeley, CA: Ten Speed Press.

Ryden, Hope. 1997. *Lily Pond: Four Years with a Family of Beavers*. New York: Lyons Press.

Savage-Rumbaugh, Sue, and Roger Lewin. 1994. *Kanzi: The Ape at the Brink of the Human Mind*. New York: John Wiley & Sons.

Schaeff, C. M., D. J. Boness, and W. D. Bowen. 1999. Female distribution, genetic relatedness, and fostering behaviour in harbor seals, *Phoca vitulina*. *Animal Behaviour* 57 (2): 427–434.

Serpell, J. 1986. *In the Company of Animals: A Study of Human-Animal Relationships*. Cambridge: Cambridge University Press.

————, ed. 1995. *The Domestic Dog*. Cambridge: Cambridge University Press.

————. 1996. Beneficial effects of pet ownership on some aspects of human health and behavior. *Journal of the Royal Society of Medicine* 84: 717–720.

Sheldrake, Rupert. 1999. *Dogs That Know When Their Owners Are Coming Home: And Other Unexplained Powers of Animals*. New York: Crown Publishers.

Slobodchikoff, C. N., Judith Kiriazis, C. Fischer, and E. Creef. 1991. Semantic information distinguishing individual predators in the alarm calls of Gunnison's prairie dogs. *Animal Behaviour* 42: 713–719.

Smyth, R. H. 1962. *Animal Habits: The Things Animals Do*. Springfield, IL: Charles C. Thomas.

Sober, Elliot, and David Sloan Wilson. 1998. *Unto Others: The Evolution and Psychology of Unselfish Behavior*. Cambridge, MA: Harvard University Press.

Steigner, B., and S. H. Steigner. 1992. *Strange Power of Pets*. New York: Donald Fine.

Steinhart, Peter. 1995. *In the Company of Wolves*. New York: Knopf.

Thomas, E. M. 1993. *The Hidden Life of Dogs*. Boston: Houghton Mifflin.

————. 1995. *The Tribe of Tiger*. Boston: Houghton Mifflin.

Van Dyk, Ann. 1991. *The Cheetahs of De Wildt*. Cape Town, South Africa: Struik Publishers (Pty) Ltd.

Vander Wall, Steven. 1990. *Food Hoarding in Animals*. Chicago: University of Chicago Press.

Watt, Ronnie. 1999. *Ten Years of Nature's Wonders*. Centurion, South Africa: Rapid Commercial Print Brokers and Publishers cc.

Weisbord, Merrily, and Kim Kachanoff. 2000. *Dogs with Jobs: Working Dogs Around the World*. New York: Pocket Books.

Weiss, Emily. 1997. Service dog selection tests: Effectiveness for dogs from animal shelters. *Applied Animal Behaviour Science* 53 (4): 297–308.

Wilkinson, Gerald S. 1984. Reciprocal food sharing in the vampire bat. *Nature* 308 (5955): 181–184.

———. 1992. Communal nursing in the evening bat. *Behavioral Ecology and Sociobiology* 31 (4): 225–235.

I am always interested in hearing about animals inspiring people, setting examples for them, or choosing to do good for them or for other animals. If you have a story that you'd like to share, you can write to me at *kvkreisler@earthlink.net* or P.O. Box 10472, Bainbridge Island, Washington 98110. Or you can reach me through my website, www.kristinvonkreisler.com (if possible, please include your address and telephone number, so I can contact you).

PHOTOGRAPHY CREDITS

About the Author

Kristin von Kreisler is a well-known animal writer and advocate. Author of *The Compassion of Animals*, she has been a staff writer for *Reader's Digest* and has written for publications including *Parade, Family Circle, Animal People, Ladies' Home Journal,* and *Glamour*. She has been a commentator on animal issues for numerous television and radio programs, a board member of the international organization In Defense of Animals, and a regular judge for the North Shore Animal League's monthly Lewyt Award for Heroic Animals. Von Kreisler lives in Woodside, California, and on Bainbridge Island, Washington.